SMOCKS
& Smocking

Smocks
and Smocking

Beverley
Marshall

 VAN NOSTRAND REINHOLD COMPANY

NEW YORK   CINCINNATI   TORONTO   LONDON   MELBOURNE

© 1980 by Beverley Marshall

First published in England in 1980 by Alphabooks, Sherborne, Dorset, England. Reprinted 1981, 1983.
U.K. ISBN 0 9506171 1 3 (cloth)
0 906670 26 8 (paper)

Special edition published by WI Books Ltd,
39 Eccleston Street, London SW1W 9 NT

ISBN 0-900556-78-1

This book was designed and produced by Alphabet and Image Ltd, Sherborne, Dorset, England

Photoset by Photosetting and Secretarial Services, Yeovil, Ltd, in Andover typeface.
Printed in the United Kingdom.

Acknowledgements

The author thanks the following people and organizations, and many others too numerous to mention, for much help with photographs, costumes, information, etc: Rosie and Susy Young, Annie Burnham, Kathleen Brabyn, Captain H. A. Cotes-James, Sue Haynes, Sue Dunne and Frances Godley; Curators of museums in Glastonbury, Abingdon, Guildford, Winchester, Brympton d'Evercy, Weybridge and Dorchester; and Reference Libraries at Yeovil and Dorchester, and the Victoria Reference Library, London. Thanks are also due for the following photographs: Alphabet and Image, pp. 5, 6, 7 right, 38 bottom, 70, 95 top, 81, 101, 102; Barnardo Publications Ltd, 7 left; Bradford Art Galleries and Museums Service, 22 bottom right; Buckinghamshire County Museum, Aylesbury, 1, 14 bottom, 16 bottom right, 22 top; Castle Gate Museum, Nottingham, 48 bottom; Crafts Advisory Committee, London, photo David Cripps, 9 bottom right; Deighton Bros Ltd, 49, 50 left; Dorset Natural History and Archaeological Society, 12 bottom; Gloucester City Museum and Art Gallery, 91 bottom; Guildford Museum, 13 top left, 25, 26 top; Harris Museum and Art Gallery, Preston, 37 top; Malcolm Henchley, 60 top; Hereford City Museum, 28 bottom, 62 bottom left; Hereford and Worcester County Museum, Hartlebury Castle, 10, 14 top, 43 top left, 61 right; Arthur Ingram, photo Malcolm Harris, 8; Alastair Lamb, 36 bottom right; Museum of London, 9 left; Luton Museum and Art Gallery, photo Bob Irons, 22 bottom left, 43 bottom right; National Museum of Wales (Welsh Folk Museum), Cardiff, 30, 31 both, 42 bottom, 62 top left; University of Reading, Museum of English Rural Life, 20, 36 top, 36 bottom left, 41 bottom; Salisbury and South Wiltshire Museum, 43 top right, 60 right; E. J. Sandell, 90; Sciaoni's Studio Ltd, London, 28 top, 33, 34, 51, 52, 69, 73, 75, 77, 79, 87, 88, 100; Stitchcraft (Condé Nast), 18; Sally Tuffin, photo Marit Lieberson, 57 right; Trustees of the Victoria and Albert Museum, London, title, 11, 13 right, 23 top, 40, 42 top; Weldon's (IPC), 95 bottom; Anna Wolsey, 43 bottom left; Woodspring Museum, Weston-super-Mare, 12 top left, 16 top left, 23 bottom, 62 bottom right. Other photographs were taken by Jeremy Marshall. All line drawings are by the author.

First published in paperback in 1981

Library of Congress Catalog Card Number 81 = 5003

ISBN 0-442-28269-9

Van Nostrand Reinhold Company
135 West 50th Street, New York, NY 10020

Cloth edition published 1980 in the United Kingdom by Alphabooks and 1981 in the United States by Van Nostrand Reinhold Company

Contents

1 Introduction

'No artistic dresser should be without a smock cut exactly like a farm labourer's' ... or a fisherman's, or an artist's, or a mother-to-be's, or a butcher or a baker's ... Good advice, this, given a century ago in a fashion magazine of 1880.

The trouble is that a century of development in the use of the word has left many people unsure of what smocks and smocking really means. The purpose of this chapter is to disentangle and define.

A smock is a garment, usually a protective over-garment, and its history is briefly described in Chapter 2. It is characteristically simply cut, with a lot of fullness and long sleeves. *Fishermen's Smocks* or *Breton Smocks Now In*, say the signs in shops catering for teenage fashion and sportswear, and the garments they refer to conform to this description. They are simply cut, with long sleeves set squarely in, similar back and front, sometimes with a boat or stand-up collar, and usually made of plain material and undecorated. They keep out the wind, and although made of strong material they are cheap to buy. *Children's Smocks* or *Smock Dresses* are the signs in other departments of clothing stores, and this time they mean pretty party clothes, usually light in weight, often made of patterned fabric, and 'smocked' here may refer to the technique of gathering material and sewing it together with special stitches to give a decorative pattern. The function of giving shape to the design sometimes shows at the wrist or the waist.

A modern plain smock protects the potter

So a 'smock' is often plain, but 'smocking' is a decoration. By combining the garment and the technique we have a decorated over-garment, and to complicate matters further there is a tradition that the decorated over-garment or 'smocked smock' is also densely embroidered in panels alongside the decorative smocking. A purist would contend that a smock is not a smock unless it is an embroidered and smocked smock. When the garment satisfies the purist, it will resemble quite closely the land-worker's smock on page 8. But every fashion designer knows that one must not be confined by tradition or convention, and by selecting and combining techniques and styles, something new can be created to make you look good in the world of today.

This is the great asset of smocks and smocking: they make people look good. Even the modern man who says 'I would not be seen dead in a thing

A child's party dress that can be bought today, beautifully smocked by hand.

like that!' meaning the densely embroidered facade of the garment, will happily wear a stylish canvas smock on his sailing boat, and the embroidery which separates the smocked man from the smocked boy appears again on the glamorous evening clothes of the modern woman.

This book is not aiming to resuscitate a moribund rustic fashion; there are plenty of others which do this, and spokes in the wheel of fashion are usually brushed aside. The King's Road trade will always draw from traditional working wear — whether it be commando-type reinforced sweaters or miners' rivetted levis — whatever functional details make the wearer look good. This is the role of the modern smock.

'Fishermen's smocks have universal appeal for boys, girls, men and women ...' Barnardo's mail order catalogue

2 The rise and fall of the

Shepherd's smock-frock, nineteenth century.

An early sixteenth century *Book of Husbandrie* gives an alarming account of the duties expected of the wife by a farmer. Besides attending to the tasks related to feeding and looking after him and his offspring, she must be ready, at the 'beginning of March, to make her garden and get as many good seeds and herbs as she needeth, sow hemp to make sheets, bed-clothes and smocks and other such necessaries.' This kindly gentleman goes on to say she should always be prepared for a pastime and need not ever be idle! The smocks he mentioned would be her own undergarments.

From the Middle Ages to the eighteenth century a 'smock' was the name given to a woman's undergarment worn next to the skin and made of linen. Confusingly, this garment then became known as a 'shift' and later the French term 'chemise' seemed more appropriate for these beautifully embroidered items of underwear.

The cut of the chemise was very similar to the early protective garb of the land worker and consisted simply of two rectangles joined together with spaces for head and arms. Since this was clothing at its most basic, it was usual for smock-type garments to be found in every period and country and worn by all social groups as outer clothing or underclothing.

The land worker's protective smock was worn throughout western Europe; it varied in decorative detail from country to country, but the cut and style bore a close resemblance to what in England became known as the smock-frock. In Holland it was a *wit-kiel*, meaning white smock, and the Italians wore a *gabbanella*, a poor man's frock, in the sixteenth century. In Scandinavia the *skyta* was the name for a similar garment, and the German *kittel* was made of dark coarse linen. Many modern versions of these peasant garments are still worn in blouse and shirt form — the similarity of cut is easily recognizable — the most

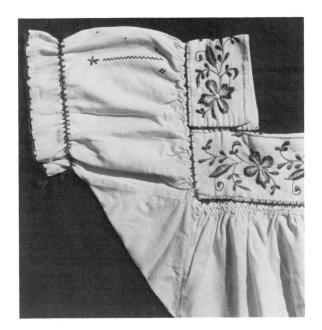

A present day embroidered blouse, cousin to the smock, from Kashmir.

Smock

Early seventeenth-century finely embroidered 'chemise' of white linen, precursor of the rural smock. 'Stript for the race how bright she did appear, No covering hid her feet, her bosom bare.' This poem of 1714 is describing the smock race. At Whitsun, Shrove Tuesday or other public holidays, sporting events were once held in which the prize for the ladies's race was a fine linen smock, in this case an undergarment, the cause of much misunderstanding.

The male equivalent of the chemise was the shirt. It was generously cut with the voluminous fabric embroidered, and finely pleated at the neck into a small band or stand-up collar.

Clothes and the life styles that created them cannot be put into tidy categories for the convenience of documentation. The smock is especially difficult to organize into neat regional or occupational pigeon-holes since it is far

familiar of all is the shirt of the Hungarian folk costume which for centuries has combined the basic elements of smock cut with ornate decoration and smocking.

removed from the extravagant dress of privileged society which has been well documented. Thus we know very little of the makers or wearers of agricultural smocks, although many of the garments are stowed away in our museums.

Their value as objects of social history was at first unrecognized — it was their picturesque qualities that prompted their preservation. But now interest in the life style of the nineteenth-century

A white linen smock from Diss in Norfolk, made during the first half of the nineteenth century. Embroidered in a variety of feather stitch, and smocked in trellis, rope and cable stitches.

A Daguerrotype of a young man wearing a smock of the 1870s.

working man is stimulated, and unanswerable questions are being asked. Unfortunately, the nineteenth-century writer who tried to describe the everyday life of the poor knew as little of manual work as the labourer did of writing. Photography was in its infancy and early examples imitated paintings rather than depicting life as it was. The true facts about the agricultural smock's history have thus disappeared with their makers and wearers, now dead seventy years or more. Their descendants often discarded worthless and work garments, modern housing and values allowing no corners for junk. At best the smock was donated to the local museum with little or no information about its origin. Local dramatic societies also benefitted from kindly but misguided donors, and the smock was worn in amateur theatricals as a sartorial symbol to the verge of disintegration.

The word 'frock' added in the nineteenth century had long been associated with an over-garment worn by men — the ecclesiastical connotation being the most obvious, for an unfrocked priest

was one deprived of his religious status. The composite term 'smock-frock' aptly describes the voluminous over-garment worn by the country labourer. It was constructed from a series of rectangles of tough home-spun and hand-woven linen and it proved excellent protection against the English climate in the days before rubber or synthetic fabrics. The fullness of the garment, making it stand away from the body of the wearer, would provide insulation for warmth in winter and keep him cool in the summer. The decorative stitchery on the gathered material had a two-fold purpose — it held the material together and also gave it elasticity. The surface embroidery not only displayed the skill and imagination of the maker, but in some instances provided further protection and padding on the shoulder and chest areas. Thread the same colour as the fabric was usually employed for both the decorative surface embroidery and the decorative lines of stitchery in the smocking. The result was a garment that fulfilled its main purpose as a warm working costume of strength and durability, very suitable for the manual worker before the age of

mechanization. The term agricultural labourer can embrace farmers, shepherds, carters, woodmen, cowmen and drovers. All these and others adopted the smock-frock as their unique protective garb from the late eighteenth century to the eventual demise of the self-supporting village community at the end of the nineteenth. Although relatively short-lived, no other occupational garment in the history of costume reached such perfection. The apron was in use before the smock, but never achieved refinement or such splendour of decoration.

The purpose of the smock varied with district, occupation and occasion. It was worn by the farm labourer either because his everyday clothes merited protection or because they were so shabby they needed hiding. For shepherds on wintry hillsides the smock was an ideal protection, sometimes improved by an additional layer in the form of a long cape, waterproofed with pitch or oil, and it is in the shepherd's occupation that the smock blossomed into the beautifully decorated garment of a century ago. In some places it was

usual for shepherds to be buried in their smocks. This was an extension of the widespread custom of laying a piece of sheep's wool in the coffin to excuse the shepherd his deficiencies in church attendance by the demands of his calling.

Smocks documented as 'worn by carters, waggoners or drovers' were sometimes shorter than the shepherds' garments, but almost equalled them in their decoration. They were worn as a dust-coat by the carter, who did much of his travelling when the tracks were dusty and dry.

The travelling man, exposed to the weather, was probably the first to take over the woman's undergarment design for his outer protection. As early as the mid eighteenth century Henry Purefoy, in the *Purefoy Letters*, asks his tailor to 'bring the coachman a linnen frock to put over his clothes when he rubs his horses down.' Dirty jobs have always needed overalls, and there are records of butchers and bakers, cider makers and brewers all using the smock-frock for protective wear, like Mr Marsh the fishmonger, shown overleaf.

11

Mr Marsh, fishmonger of Weston-super-Mare, 1850.

In *The Dress and Manners of the English*, published in 1813, the smock is amongst those garments which 'may be said to represent the usual dress of the farmer's servants in the southern parts of the country.' By mid century, the agricultural smock was worn by workers in the field, and this included the child labourers, whose smocks were miniatures of the adult version.

In his novel *Under the Greenwood Tree* of 1871, Thomas Hardy, sensitive recorder of rural life, describes the materials of which labourers' smocks were made: 'Some were as usual in snow white smocks of Russian duck and some in whitey brown ones of drabbet.' The smock of the mid nineteenth century was often made of bleached glazed linen, known as 'duck', a relatively fine fabric particularly suited to neat stitchery. Other smocks were made of hardwearing coarse linen which was unbleached, home-spun and hand-woven, and ideal for the practical protective garment. 'Holland' or linen 'drill' was much used in smock-making, and this was unbleached cloth with a familiar twill weave, originally imported into Britain from the Netherlands (hence its name). A heavy cotton twill, similar in appearance to Holland, was the 'drabbet' Hardy refers to, usually beige, fawn or greenish-grey in colour. Several dark brownish-black smocks are documented in British museums, chiefly from the Surrey and Sussex areas. They are made from linen and have been steeped in boiled linseed oil to improve their protective qualities. The result was a rather stiff, shiny garment, extremely waterproof and very warm, which required no laundering other than a wipe down. The linen unfortunately deteriorated rather more quickly as a result of the action of linseed on the fibres, and there may have been many more black and dark brown smocks than we have evidence for today. The embroidery on these garments was greatly enhanced by a dark background; the embroidery thread was tightly spun and often waxed, so that it did not absorb the oil so readily as the fabric. This oiling process dates back to the thirteenth century,

Dorsetshire peasantry of 1846. The men are wearing round smocks, hob-nail boots and billy-cock hats, the boy from the farmstead is wearing a replica of his father's outfit.

12

Smocked boys in the late nineteenth century, helping to run the farm.

and was similar to the technique used by the fishermen on their oilskins.

Fawn or whitish-brown smocks are sometimes found in museums, but more frequently occurring are smocks in white and off-white. Thomas Hardy, who unwittingly is to provide us with the best social documentary of the garment, as we shall see later, gives us an important clue to the reason for this when, in *Under the Greenwood Tree*, a wedding guest appears wearing 'a long white smock of pillow-case cut'.

The working garment was supplemented by a 'best' smock, more highly decorated, used for weddings, funerals, Sundays and special occasions, and almost always white. It is these special smocks which have in the main survived, and many are illustrated here. In museums they are often documented as 'wedding smocks' and were traditional wedding attire for both groom and guests at English country weddings. In Surrey the custom was for a bride to work a beautiful smock as a love token for her future husband, and some of the symbolic embroidery described in Chapter 5 may have originated here. In some villages, sets of white or black smocks were made for coffin bearers, giving a ghostly uniformity to the men without requiring them to change their clothes beneath. These garments were the property of the church and like the choir boy's surplice were well laundered and starched. Significantly, the last smocks to be worn for a practical purpose were those worn by such coffin bearers in Sussex and Hampshire, a custom that survived until the 1930s.

ABOVE An early nineteenth-century wedding smock and LEFT an oiled smock, both from Sussex.

Labourers would wear their best smocks for the annual Hiring fairs in county towns, usually held after harvesting at Michaelmas. In the days of semi-literacy, working people had to present themselves to potential employers without previous reference or correspondence; labourers were engaged on a yearly basis on 'face' value. A good clean smock would help this first impression. The country fair dates back to the fourteenth century, and continues today, often with a local name, though it no longer serves as an employment exchange.

13

Bewdley 1875. Farmers come into town on market days in smocks and top hats.

The usual scene at a Victorian country fair was a large crowd of workers, mainly agricultural, congregated in groups. It was important to them as well as to the employers that their occupations could be easily recognized or identified by what they wore or carried. According to Thomas Hardy, 'carters and waggoners had a piece of whipcord twisted round their hats; thatchers wore a fragment of woven straw and shepherds carried their crooks.' Hob-nail boots were an essential accessory for the smock-clad labourer, so too was the 'billy-cock' hat. A brightly-coloured neck scarf made of finely woven wool was usually worn with the smock, but the accessories seem to have many regional variations. Trousers were made of 'fustian' or 'moleskin': a strong twilled cotton with a smooth matt surface favoured by the labourer for its resemblance to their earlier leather breeches. They were hitched up under the knee by a leather strap or simply a piece of string, good for preventing field mice and insects from running up the wearer's legs. Crude 'cords' were also worn, said to be soaked in horse urine to matt the fibres of the fabric and thus prolong wear. White cords, well scrubbed and as wholesome as the proverbial scrubbed table top in the cottager's kitchen, were worn in some areas.

Smocks were given away as prizes to the winner of a ploughing match or similar event at the local fair. These coveted garments were often fine examples of the smock-maker's art. A smock would cost between nine and eighteen shillings (45-90 pence or $1-2) to buy, depending on the quality — expensive, as smocks were worn by the lowest wage earners and this could equal one or two weeks' earnings. It is not surprising that many smocks were made in the home and were passed down from one generation to the next, with only minor alterations.

Farmers at the Victorian Hirings would not wear smocks themselves, and Thomas Hardy, this time in *Far From the Madding Crowd*, gives an indication of how the smock was sliding down the social scale. Gabriel Oak, having failed to get a job as a bailiff or farm superintendent, 'exchanged his overcoat for a shepherd's regulation smock-frock'. However ornate the smock, it would mark him as one of the lower orders.

The best example of the agricultural labour force wearing their Sunday best comes from a report in *The Times* of 13 June, 1851, describing a visit to the Great Exhibition at Crystal Palace:

A white linen prize smock won by a farmer's son from Buckinghamshire for a ploughing match in 1890.

The rise and fall of the smock

A remarkable feature of yesterday's experience in the interior of the Exhibition was the appearance there, at an early hour, of nearly 800 agricultural labourers and countryfolk from the neighbourhood of Godstone in Surrey, headed by the clergymen of the parishes to which they respectively belonged ... the men wore their smartest smock-frocks and the women their best Sunday dresses and more perfect specimens of rustic attire, rustic faces and rustic manners could hardly be produced from any part of England.

The rustics, it seems, behaved themselves to the satisfaction of the organizers, who had expected them instead to vandalize the machines and carve their names on the woodwork.

When it is remembered that Prince Albert's aim for the Exhibition was the marriage of high art and mechanical skill, it can be seen as a turning point in the history of the smock itself. The machine age introduced farm implements that on the one hand endangered the lives of the smock-frocked labour forces — the unconfined looseness of the garment was a positive hazard near the moving parts of the machinery — and on the other

Part of a smock made by cottagers for Messrs. Harris & Tomkins of Abingdon, exhibited at the Great Exhibition of 1851 and again in 1951. The elaborate embroidery portrayed the fashionable themes of universal peace and prosperity; wheat sheaves, hearts, beehives and flowers feature on the chest in circular motifs; the lowest circle had two figures, possibly Agriculture and Success personified.

by more speedily carrying out their function deprived the labourers of their livelihood. The portable steam thresher was an obvious example: a week's labouring for many hands was worked by this monster in one full day. Redundancy was widespread and better communication between town and country began to lure youths from their rural backgrounds to the cities. None of them wished to be associated with the simple ways of parents and grand-parents. The cities meant higher wages, better jobs and work for the redundant. Their indifference and change of attitude towards the smock was partially due to a genuine fear of ridicule and even victimization by their smart city contemporaries. In the towns the smock was already associated with the street vendor or hawker, who sold pegs, mats and other wares from baskets door to door, and kept other produce such as game birds in his smock pockets. The smock was also the uniform of the 'poor-house' child, and as such it would be cheaply made and unadorned.

A slow decline in the quality of the fabric and the decoration of the garment may well have dated from the Great Exhibition, because the very mechanization which the event was to celebrate made it easier for a factory industry in ready-made smocks to develop.

A street vendor selling pottery, 1839.

15

The rise and fall of the smock

Manufactured smocks were a characteristic of the later nineteenth century, and first in the field was a family firm at Newark upon Trent which made the characteristic blue Newark Frock, popular in the Midland counties of England, and using indigo dye from Coventry. Because of the cheapness, blue had long been the colour associated with house-servants, apprentices and other employees of the upper classes in Britain. The example of the Newark Frock shows, however, that it was well

disguised himself 'in a gathered smock-frock, such as was worn only by the most old fashioned of the labourers.'

By a curious twist, at this very point in time, the garment achieved a new role, tracing a familiar pattern in the history of fashion. As it was discarded by the field labourer and was seen less as a working garment, so it was adopted by the fashion conscious, the trend-setters of the late

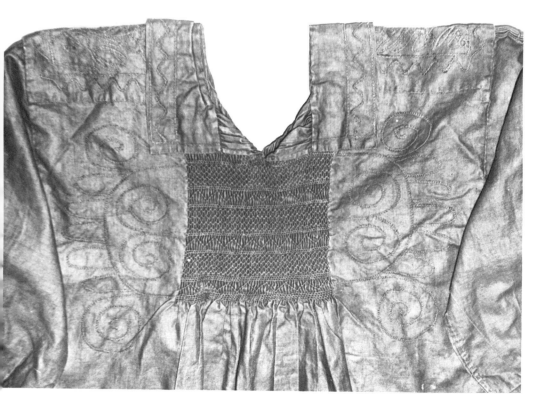

LEFT A dark blue Newark-Frock from Derby. The attractive embroidery design was printed from metal blocks and stitched by outworkers. BELOW A ready-made smock made by a cottager for a draper's shop in Buckinghamshire.

made and decorated, and at the height of its success there were ten smock manufacturing companies in Newark. The ready-cut garments from the factory would be smocked and embroidered by cottage out-workers, then assembled by machine back at the factory or warehouse. Most smock or 'slop' vendors at fairs would have ready-made stock from such factories, though some smocks were still entirely made by hand by cottagers for a local draper. Mid nineteenth century records from a village in Wiltshire describe an industrious housewife who made smocks from three yards of holland at 4½d (2 pence, 5 cents) a yard, walked eight miles to deliver them to the local town and was then paid 9d (4 pence, 10 cents) per smock for her labour.

By the 1880s this ill-rewarded hand labour was replaced by the factory garment, and a decade later these too went into decline. Thomas Hardy, who had celebrated the universality of the smock in his early novels, wrote in *Tess of the D'Urbervilles* in 1891 of how Alec D'Urberville, to surprise Tess,

16

nineteenth century. The friends of Oscar Wilde, William Morris and other revolutionaries, promoted the 'smock' as a healthy aesthetic garment and as a protest against the opulence of the manufacturers of the machine age. Its unconfined fabric made it a practical style for the fashionable game of lawn tennis. The plans of the Arts and Crafts Movement and the philanthropic ideals of influential ladies to patronize the country-folk never really caught on, but even so their good intentions did not escape the satirical eye of *Punch*. From that day onwards, the cartoonist's concept of the bohemian artist always shows him in his studio clad in a smock, usually incongruously wearing a beret.

The more commercial world of fashion, however, was at work on the basic design and the smocking technique. *The Ladies World* magazine of 1880 illustrated 'The Mab Smock', designed for Messrs Liberty of Regent Street, London, and made of light blue cashmere embroidered in silk. Liberty's did not actually make clothes themselves, but their fabrics dominated the art world of the mid and late nineteenth century for both quality and style. Umritza cashmere was used for the Mab smock for, in common with their silk fabrics, it was ideally suited to fine hand smocking. In 1887, Weldon's published illustrated practical guides which informed and instructed the middle-class ladies on the art of smocking. Their leisure hours and busy hands were occupied applying the embroidery technique to a variety of garments for women and children. 'Tea gowns' and the 'Garibaldi' jacket had fullness controlled by

A child's pure silk dress of 1895; the lace is machine-made and the smocked bodice fastens down the back. The smocking and other hand embroidery techniques relate incongruously to the decoration of the smock-frock.

Liberty's have always had a reputation for exquisitely hand-decorated garments. In the early twenties classic-style blouses advertised in their catalogue were hand smocked and made of silk.

17

A smocked blouse of 1935 made in silk crêpe-de-chine.

elaborate smocking. Smocking was also adapted for many household items and even to such trivialities as the handkerchief sachets and 'bedroom tidies'. Weldon's, through their magazines, continued to make smock patterns available to the twentieth century housewife, for her nightwear and her children's clothes. They were joined by many other publications. Although smocked and in some instances called 'smock' the garments were nothing like the agricultural garment of fifty years before.

Specialist magazines like *The Embroiderer* and later *Stitchcraft* popularized the subject during the thirties and forties, introducing many new and inventive stitches.

Since the late forties many reputable children's wear manufacturers have produced dresses and romper suits which have imitation smocking applied by machine, so that a hint of the original technique is available today in every multiple store. More recently, the *Golden Hands* craft magazine has attractively brought smocking right up to date.

The future of the technique is therefore secure, but the traditional garment has also been revived from time to time since its demise in the nineteenth century. Most notable was the work of Sarah Bere, wife of the vicar of Bere Regis in Dorset, who established in the first decade of this century a small revival industry in her village to make replicas of the original garments, before the First World War distracted her attention into helping the war effort. Her son Rennie is photographed here in one of the garments she made. The value of these revivals is mainly in the concern for the authentic embroidery patterns which flank the smocking and are described in Chapter 5.

Today craft shops everywhere encourage and promote the appreciation of hand-made items and are prepared to stock and sell replicas of the traditional garments. Reproductions of the nineteenth century farm labourer's smock-frock have also become popular subjects for competitions, and the survival of all the traditional designs can safely be left in the capable and fastidious hands of the British Women's Institute.

A revival smock made by Mrs Sarah Bere is worn here by her son Rennie before the First World War.

A present-day revival smock with Dorset feather stitch embroidery.

3 Smock types and variations

In the later nineteenth century the hedger, shown in the photograph below, wears a hessian sack, with holes for his head and arms. A similar sack conversion is practised today by farm workers, for protection, but these sacks are made of polythene and tied with plastic baler twine!

This is the basic element of the smock: two similar pieces of material, joined at the shoulders and sides. It is the tabard worn by Chaucerian characters in the fourteenth century. Two more rectangles, folded lengthways into sleeves, were added to make the smock. The pattern of the nineteenth century smock-frock varied from one area to another, but a similarity of shape and decoration is often apparent in a collection of smocks housed in a provincial museum, and the garment can be seen as belonging to one of three main types.

The round smock

The round or true smock is the most widely recognized type, but within its type it had the greatest variety of styles. The typical pattern is shown alongside. It has a deep rectangular yoke of double thickness fabric. It is a reversible smock, with a short opening at the front and back of the neck, just sufficient to allow the wearer to pull the garment over his head. The smaller the opening the more value the garment had as a protection against the hazards of the labourer's occupation, protecting the clothes beneath from everything from straw to cow dung. The generous cut prevented excessive wear in any one area, and the garment could be reversed, thus distributing the wear evenly. This would be a popular feature, also delaying the need to wash the garment until it was dirty on both sides.

Many round smocks, however, did not stick perfectly to the same-back-and-front principle, having openings down the 'front' into the smocked area. Most openings were quite short, with three or four buttons, but others extended to the base of the smocking panel or even below. These longer openings were faced out with a strip of fabric to accommodate buttons and buttonholes. Often many buttons very close together were used to ensure complete protection

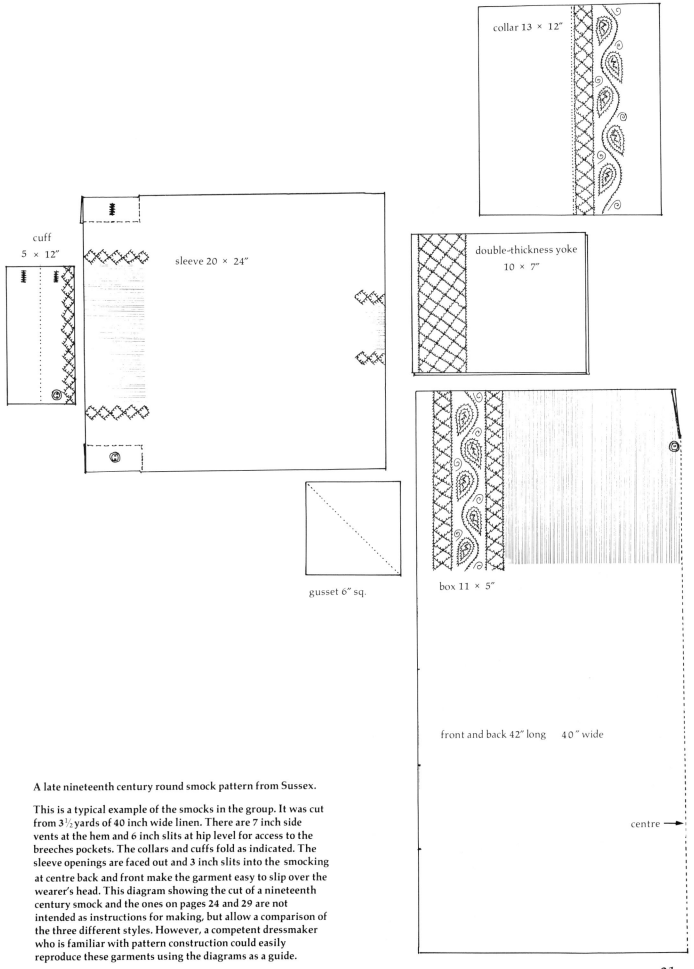

collar 13 × 12″

cuff
5 × 12″

sleeve 20 × 24″

double-thickness yoke
10 × 7″

gusset 6″ sq.

box 11 × 5″

front and back 42″ long   40″ wide

centre →

A late nineteenth century round smock pattern from Sussex.

This is a typical example of the smocks in the group. It was cut from 3½ yards of 40 inch wide linen. There are 7 inch side vents at the hem and 6 inch slits at hip level for access to the breeches pockets. The collars and cuffs fold as indicated. The sleeve openings are faced out and 3 inch slits into the smocking at centre back and front make the garment easy to slip over the wearer's head. This diagram showing the cut of a nineteenth century smock and the ones on pages 24 and 29 are not intended as instructions for making, but allow a comparison of the three different styles. However, a competent dressmaker who is familiar with pattern construction could easily reproduce these garments using the diagrams as a guide.

The round smock, sometimes called a 'true' smock, worn by Thomas Pitkin of Swanbourne in Buckinghamshire.

of the wearer's chest, with no holes to gape to the wind. The short openings were not faced; the fabric was neatly turned back and hemmed firmly and the button and buttonhole worked within the smocked area, or on the collar itself.

The usual collar for the round smock comprised two rectangles of cloth, each folded in half with the uppermost section embroidered. This collar, which stood high into the neck of the wearer, was not very comfortable and to overcome this some smocks had the four corners of the collar buttoned down to the garment.

Many shapes and sizes of collar feature on the smocks with a centre-front opening. It gave more freedom of design as the collar no longer needed to be split at the centre back. Some smocks had small collars cut all in one piece. But the flat collar as shown on pages 33 and 34 appeared to be the most popular for the round smock, occasionally extending into a cape-like feature, more usually associated with the coat smock (see page 28).

The decoration of the round smock was its most characteristic feature, particularly the surface embroidery with its scrolls, floral and geometric shapes worked in the 'box', on the collar and on the shoulders. The so-called box was the area either side of the smocked panel and it varied in width and depth. But not all round smocks had this added decoration.

LEFT **A neat one-piece collar is the distinctive feature of this smock from Stewkley in Buckinghamshire. It is made of brown linen and, from the detailed embroidery of the 'box' and the brass buttons, is dated about 1840.** ABOVE **An ornate North Country smock from Bradford,** *c.* **1850, three buttons to each collar flap.**

A heavy cotton round smock from Berkshire, with yoke modified to slope with the shoulders.

These garments were usually worn knee-length. Some had long side vents with small gussets to strengthen the opening, and a similar gusset was occasionally used on the sleeve opening. The deep rectangular yoke that gave this smock its ungainly angular shape appears modified in some garments of the late nineteenth century. It was less deep, and sloped with the shoulders. A good example of the modified shape is seen above ·

A shepherd's round smock from Somerset with an unusually small collar buttoned to the smocking.

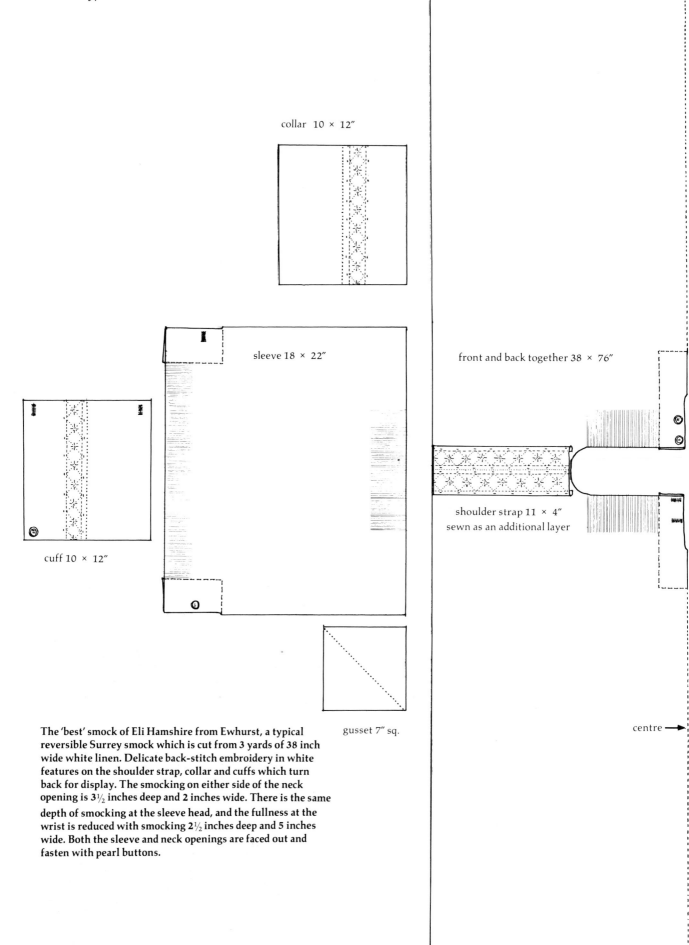

collar 10 × 12"

sleeve 18 × 22"

front and back together 38 × 76"

shoulder strap 11 × 4"
sewn as an additional layer

cuff 10 × 12"

gusset 7" sq.

centre ➝

The 'best' smock of Eli Hamshire from Ewhurst, a typical reversible Surrey smock which is cut from 3 yards of 38 inch wide white linen. Delicate back-stitch embroidery in white features on the shoulder strap, collar and cuffs which turn back for display. The smocking on either side of the neck opening is 3½ inches deep and 2 inches wide. There is the same depth of smocking at the sleeve head, and the fullness at the wrist is reduced with smocking 2½ inches deep and 5 inches wide. Both the sleeve and neck openings are faced out and fasten with pearl buttons.

The 'Surrey' smock

The shirt-like character of the 'Surrey' smock gave it a distinctive appearance which was immediately recognizable. Its pattern is shown left. It is mainly associated with the county of Surrey south-west of London, and this is how it acquired its name. Early nineteenth-century references to smocks are usually to this type, and William Cobbett in his *Rural Rides* tells us of Surrey children clad in smocks as early as 1770. The Surrey smock was worn well into the twentieth century. It had a narrow single-thickness shoulder strap, sewn along the top of the garment as an additional layer, and it extended well over the shoulder. The panels of smocking were usually quite small, appearing on the back and either side of the front neck opening, and on the wrists and near the head of the sleeves. The influence of this type spread to other areas of Britain. Some garments found in Devon, Somerset and other areas of Wessex had the narrow shoulder strap feature of the Surrey smock, but they were made of heavy linen and the smocked panels were deep features normally associated with the round smock.

The elegant smocks in this Surrey group were made of fine linen which lent itself to exquisite stitchery, with a lace-like quality. The majority had no elaborations or confusing symbols in the embroidery of the 'box', they simply had neat parallel rows of functional stitching worked on the shoulder strap, collar and cuff. The depth of the smocking either side of the back and front neck opening ranged between two and four inches (5 and 10 cm); often the opening exceeded this in length and additional decorative stitching was employed to strengthen the weak point at the base of the slit. The neck opening was usually faced out and it was fastened at the back and the front with from two to five buttons. Long side vents at the hem were not found on this type of smock, but slits one or two inches (2.5 or 5 cm) long were strengthened by a small rectangle of fabric as shown. Pockets were usually large openings in the side seam, with patches sewn to the underside of the garment. The characteristic long, narrow shoulder strap of the smock created the possibility of a variation in the method of cut and construction. *The Workwoman's Guide* promoted the system of the back and front body pieces cut all in one (see plan), with an elongated hole for the head

Eli Hamshire from Ewhurst wearing his everyday smock. He was a carrier or waggoner for thirty years during the mid-nineteenth century, and a liberal thinker and revolutionary writer.

opening. The shoulder strap was sewn on decoratively as an additional layer and strengthener. The reduced area of smocking at the neck made the garment very wide-shouldered, with the seam well down the upper arm of the wearer, giving the garment a decidedly droopy appearance. The short sleeve was wide with smocking at the wrist and head.

The typically shirt-like Surrey smock

The yoke on the Surrey smock is reduced to a mere shoulder strap decoratively stitched to the garment. BELOW, LEFT AND RIGHT.

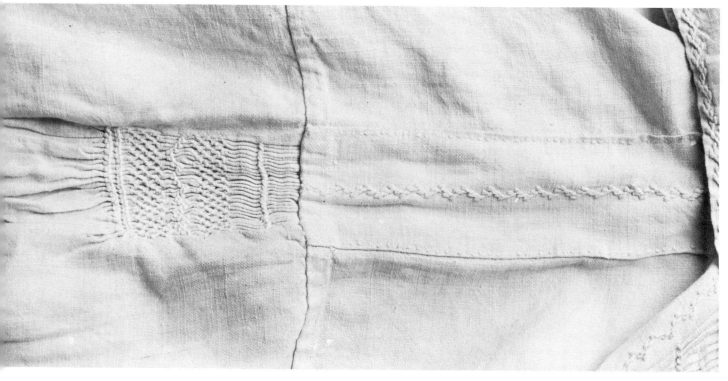

Small panels of lace-like smocking on either side of the neck opening on a Surrey smock. The zig-zag line of stitchery at the bottom of the smocking gives maximum stretch where it is most needed.

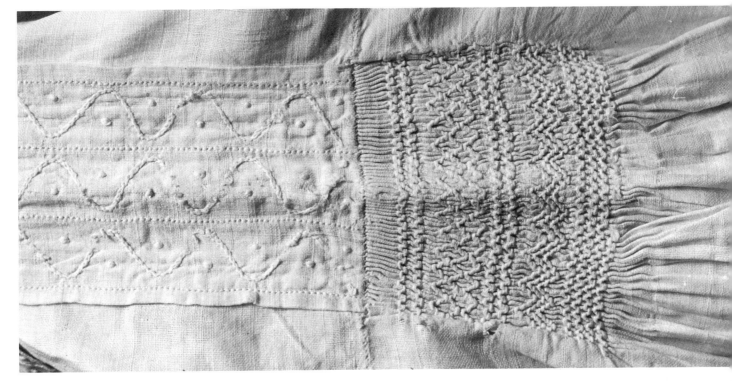

The coat smock in action

The centre-front band of a Welsh coat smock provided an additional area for decoration.

The coat smock

The coat smock was usually made of heavy linen, in a style akin to a tailored coat (see above and illustration on page 69). With many additional features and a wealth of smocking and surface embroidery, they were very heavy garments to wear and work in. They gave protection from the rains and mists of the western counties of England and the Welsh mountains and were worn mainly by shepherds in the nineteenth century. Many were well worn and patched and were obviously practical rather than 'best' garments. They were long, worn well below the knee and buttoned about two-thirds of the way down. The edge of the fabric was folded back down the centre front to form a double thickness for the buttons and buttonholes. As many as twenty-two horn buttons can be seen on one garment in the Welsh Folk Museum at St Fagans, Glamorgan. More usual were openings with eight to twelve buttons, sometimes with leaf or tree motifs embroidered in the spaces.

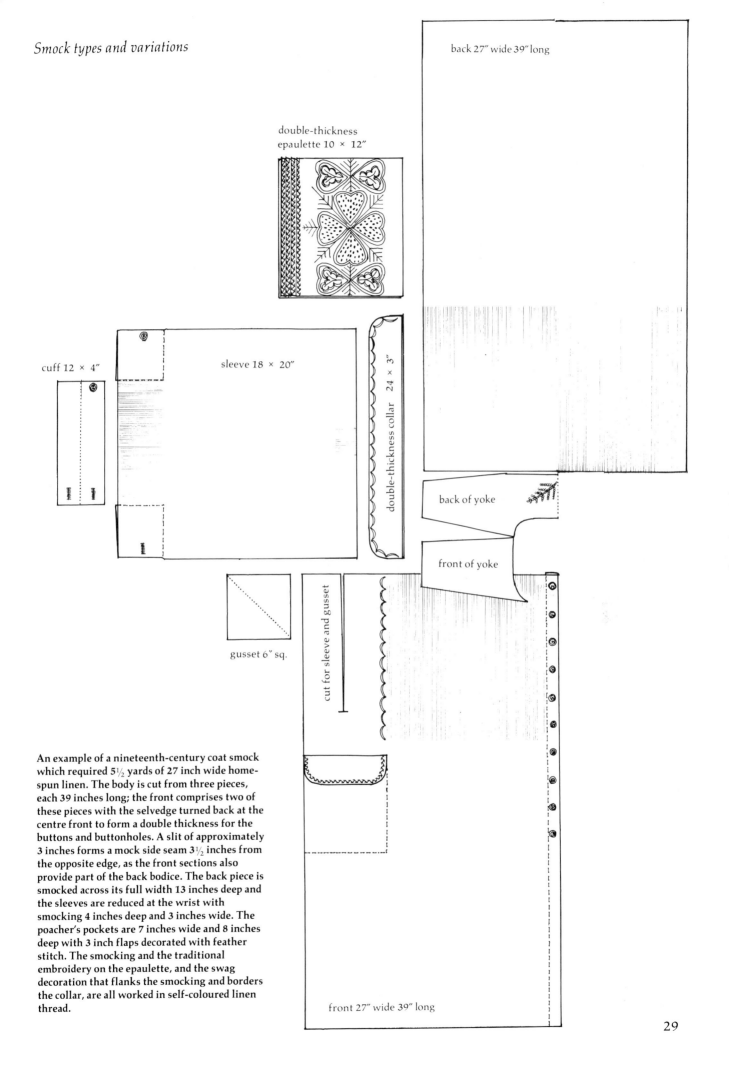

Smock types and variations

back 27" wide 39" long

double-thickness
epaulette 10 × 12"

cuff 12 × 4"

sleeve 18 × 20"

double-thickness collar   24 × 3"

back of yoke

front of yoke

gusset 6" sq.

cut for sleeve and gusset

An example of a nineteenth-century coat smock which required 5½ yards of 27 inch wide home-spun linen. The body is cut from three pieces, each 39 inches long; the front comprises two of these pieces with the selvedge turned back at the centre front to form a double thickness for the buttons and buttonholes. A slit of approximately 3 inches forms a mock side seam 3½ inches from the opposite edge, as the front sections also provide part of the back bodice. The back piece is smocked across its full width 13 inches deep and the sleeves are reduced at the wrist with smocking 4 inches deep and 3 inches wide. The poacher's pockets are 7 inches wide and 8 inches deep with 3 inch flaps decorated with feather stitch. The smocking and the traditional embroidery on the epaulette, and the swag decoration that flanks the smocking and borders the collar, are all worked in self-coloured linen thread.

front 27" wide 39" long

29

The coat smock that belonged to Ben Proctor of Chepstow is made of heavy cotton and embroidered in linen thread. The large collars are tucked at the outer edge and display the characteristic dense embroidery.

The dominant feature of many of these smocks was the large collar with tucks towards the outer edge to give it weight. These tucks were embroidered as well as the entire collar, and this was often the limit of the surface decoration in this group. Very few of these garments had the box area embroidered, but the deep panels of smocking were edged with single rows of stitching, or simple 'swags' or leaves.

Following the influence of fashionable clothing of the early nineteenth century, the large collars were made even larger and became cape-like, thus increasing the need to fix the collar to the sleeve-head or the body of the smock with buttons — a high wind on a Welsh mountain would have caused quite a problem for the wearer, and cape-like collars are often associated with smocks from Wales.

Eventually, these enormous collar flaps evolved into rectangular epaulettes of double thickness fabric. They were sewn into the front neck and

A heavy brown cotton coat smock, worn by a market gardener, with extravagant cape-like epaulettes, and embroidery filling every space.

An early nineteenth-century smock with its double cape-like protection buttoned to the shoulders.

stitched over the back shoulder. In these instances a small one-piece collar was added. Underneath all this the yoke of the coat smock was shaped to the body of the wearer and is recognizable as the sort of yoke we know today. It thus broke the rule that all the pattern pieces of the smock were cut as rectangles. It was curved at the neck, and sloped with the shoulder, and the smock was possibly more comfortable to wear for being tailored. The yoke was deep at the centre back and provided an additional area for decoration with stitchery.

Most of these coat smocks had flapped pockets, set at right angles to the body of the garment, so that exactly half of the pocket extended towards the front and half towards the back. This feature appears to be more relevant to a reversible smock, yet it was used extensively on the coat smock.

The three groups described are common types, but are not examples of hard and fast divisions of style; many of their features merge so that they can not easily be assigned to a particular group. The many variants of construction and decoration were examples of both influence and ingenuity. An additional gusset at the neck or hem may have made the garment more comfortable and practical; a special collar may have suited a special purpose.

Collars and cuffs

In all smocks the feature with the greatest diversity of shape and size was the collar. This ranged from a small one-piece style to the enormous cape-like features of the border counties of England and Wales, or the small roll

The archetypal smock, showing the good features of all three basic types — the flat decorated collar with tucks on the outer edge, deep smocking on the forearm and a decorated centre panel.

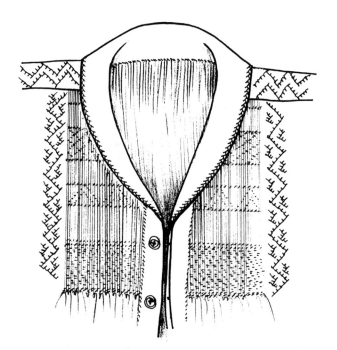

Roll collar

collar, examples of which seem to belong to the East Anglian region.

Cuffs varied only slightly, usually narrow with one button, though frequently another button on the sleeve opening was necessary, in which case the opening was faced on the inside. Some cuffs were deep and decorated and were worn turned back to display the embroidery. Smocking featured above the cuff.

Pockets

Pockets were not found on all smocks, indeed the early garments had none. Slits in the side seam for the wearer to gain access to his jacket or breeches pocket were usual and confirm that the smock was intended as outer clothing. Where there were pockets on the smock-frock they were usually large. Hardy's shepherd, Gabriel Oak, housed the necessary implements of his trade such as a marking iron and even a small teapot in his 'illimitable pockets'. The protective flaps of the

A typical cuff, with smocking and simple embroidery.

The modern smock in cotton drill. The pattern is on page 76, and the instructions for making start on page 80.

'poacher's pockets' would prevent chaff or hay from getting in and would help to hide the more bulky 'perks' of the countryside — such flaps would be buttoned down. Patch pockets were less popular on adults' garments, but were frequently found on early children's smocks.

Neck opening

The length of neck opening helps to determine the type of smock and the purpose for which it was worn. The reversible smock had a slit centre back and front of about two inches (5 cm). The coat-type smock was open right down the front, but many had openings ranging between these two extremes. Fly-front openings gave protection for the buttons which would catch in the sheep's wool or the briars of the hedgerow, and they featured on many shepherds' smocks.

TOP **The collar and fly-front opening of an unusually crude smock.**

ABOVE **The popular link button opening of a round smock.**

Special forms

Smocks devoid of smocking have aroused little interest in the past. However, they are still widely worn and now called 'fishermen's smocks'. Some early garments had smocking on the sleeves and decorated collars, but the absence of the smocked centre back and front panels is notable.

Cotton smock or 'fugu' from northern Ghana, made of narrow strips, with parallel tucking.

Only a few examples survive of this uncluttered breed of smock, as its simplicity seemed not to merit preservation.

A typical ceremonial smock from Preston in Lancashire, with
fine embroidery on the front replacing the smocking. Existing
examples are usually in good condition, as they were often
worn only once.

A tailored smock with parallel tucks instead of smocking RIGHT
Back view.

Another type of garment was cut like a smocked
coat, but with large parallel tucks instead of
smocking stitched down from yoke to waist.
These tucks provided padding for the chest and
the garment had a smart tailored appearance.
Another smock, similarly cut but without the
tucks, had the fullness of the bodice gathered into
the collar. It was machine-made in the late
nineteenth century and apart from sparse
smocking at the cuff and sleeve-head it had very
little decoration. In another case, a very short
smock was worn by a 'beater' in Somerset, and

was no doubt more practical with the fullness neatly contained at hip level. It had a silhouette like that of a modern anorak, which is often the garment worn by game beaters today.

Many of the smocks that were made for celebrations or festivals have survived in good condition, while others led a more purposeful life. Smocks made specially for ceremonial occasions often lack the fullness, the front opening and even the smocking. The large flat area at the front of the garment lent itself to the embroidering of a motif or crest and a roll collar helped to draw attention to the design. This style was well distributed throughout Britain, some with the Prince of Wales fleur-de-lys crest.

Other irregular examples of the smock-frock come to light from time to time, their original date and purpose remaining a mystery, each having a story to tell. One unique garment appeared in an auction sale room at Dorchester, undocumented. It was hardly worn, made of drabbet and lavishly decorated. The sleeves were its most unusual feature, without cuff, smocking or gusset.

An unusual smock with the appearance of a decorated overall.

A white smock was once the standard uniform of a game-beater to protect him from being shot. This unique smock, with the fullness gathered into the waist, would keep him warmer than most.

The condition of old smocks in museums and private collections can sometimes tell something about their history. Garments have been discovered badly stained and worn through natural wear, often beautifully repaired, sometimes crudely patched. Where a different fabric has been used it is likely that the repair was carried out by the next generation of wearers and not by the original maker. Alterations provide evidence that the garment was a 'hand-down' and feature not only simple shortening of sleeves and frock, but occasionally replaced cuffs and other worn parts. The smocking stitches were vulnerable and in some garments the threads have broken from the constant strain of dressing. The embroidery on many smocks has worn away from the continual rubbing of a wooden yoke or implement. Not surprisingly the shoulder area of some smocks was lined in a coarse woollen fabric, both to reduce friction and to provide cushioning against heavily-loaded shoulder packs. All these acquired features bring the smock to life; the wear on a cuff or shoulder may tell us how a particular task was performed, or a patch above the pocket gives us a clue to what was housed in it.

Many preserved garments were clearly unworn, others show signs of very little wear, as if they were preserved for posterity before their newness had been taken away. The unworn items could have been the sample garments of the professional smock-maker of the early nineteenth century, or old hand-made stock that had outlived demand in drapers' shops early this century. The modern collector, having learned about the history and common types of traditional smock, can understand a good deal about the garments he has before him from the condition, shape, material, embroidery and even the transfer lines below the patterning.

Fabrics and cut

Before machine-produced fabrics were available to the rural working classes, the fabric was hand woven from home-spun yarn. Therefore the width of the fabric would be determined by the width of the loom, which rarely exceeded twenty-seven inches (69 cm). Many smocks used three widths of fabric for the body area, butt-joined down the selvedges with tiny oversewing stitches: obviously the woven width was inadequate to accommodate the size of the wearer or the type of smock required.

With the advance of textile technology the machine loom made fabrics available for all — the greatest influence on fashion in history. Linen holland and cotton drabbet were mass-produced at more practical widths and were employed in smock making at home and in the 'trade'.

The need to utilize every inch of the fabric for economy is well expressed in the traditional smock, cut from a series of rectangles so that little or no wastage would occur. The assembling process would be well within the capabilities of the average farm labourer's wife. No curves meant no difficult shaping or construction and the smock would be cut 'by eye'; paper patterns were not necessary nor were they available. The only measurement needed would be the required length of the smock; this varied from 28 to 52 inches (71-132 cm) depending on the height of the man and the style of the garment.

It is generally accepted that the measurement from the back neck to the hem of the smock was trebled to give the full amount of fabric needed. A reasonable assessment for garments today made of fabric 36 inches (91 cm) wide. Two lengths

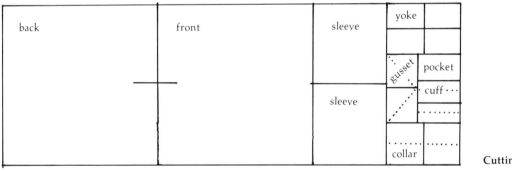

Cutting plan

Fleur-de-lys embroidered on a ceremonial smock

would have provided the back and front body sections; the third length would be halved, with one piece halved again across the width for two sleeves, and the remaining fabric would accommodate the collar, cuffs, yokes and gussets. This method of cutting, in which all the seams were on the straight grain or parallel to the selvedges, made the method of joining two pieces together quite simple, and maximum use could be made of the uncut or selvedge edge of the fabric. On a hand-woven fabric the edges would fray easily, and some method of seam finish or encasement of the raw edges would be necessary where there was no selvedge. The 'flat' seam or 'run and fell' was commonly used. With the introduction of machines to assemble the garments this method was still employed to give strength and neatness, and the same practical seam finish is used today down the legs of our jeans.

4 Smock, smocking, smocked

If 'smocking' is a legacy from the garment of the nineteenth-century field labourer, it is now the name given to the method of gathering together any width of material into regular folds and securing these folds with stitchery, which gives a unique resilience to the work and makes its own decoration. It has evolved from the need to control the fullness of the garment, make it fit snugly from the shoulder to waist and on the fore-arm, and to give maximum freedom to the limbs.

The technique has been practised since the fourteenth century: medieval peasant women were illustrated in the Luttrell Psalter of 1340 wearing long aprons (barm cloths) embroidered at the waist, and featuring a geometric design which contained the fullness of the fabric. The pleats or organized folds of fabric that preceded smocking are evident in portraits of the Renaissance period.

Wobourn sheepshearing, by George Garrard, 1811. Detail.

'Interior of an alehouse kitchen', George Morland, 1763-1804.

Durer's self-portraits clearly show a pre-smocking effect on his shirts. Other late Gothic paintings portray the embellishment of the headdress, sleeve-heads and necklines of garments, with finely pleated silk reticulated in gold and silver. There are numerous portraits by Holbein of dignitaries wearing pleated shirts with latticed decoration at the neck. These portraits were generally executed in great detail, since the artist was expected to convey the status of the sitter, but unfortunately the method of stitching used on the extravagant garments was not defined clearly enough to show how the gathers were secured.

Once the effect of organized folds had become an established fashion the next development was the inevitable decoration of the 'reeds' or 'tubes' of pleating. This provided an elasticity that ordinary pleats or tucks could not give, and it was this property which made and still makes smocking suitable for garments worn by energetic children and active adults.

Neither eighteenth-century references to the countryman's frock or 'slop', nor the drawings by artists of rural scenes, describe or illustrate the protective garment as being decorated or 'smocked'. The smock appears frequently in paintings of rural scenes as plain and practical, with ample fullness at the neck and shoulders, as in George Morland's painting of the interior of an alehouse kitchen. Yet twenty years on, the shepherds in George Garrard's engraving of Wobourn Sheep Fair clearly wear smocks decorated as we know them today. Garrard's

Smock, smocking, smocked

technique may well have been more suitable for illustrating detail than Morland's brush and oil technique. It was no coincidence that as the shirt of the late eighteenth-century nobleman became less ornate, the 'slop' of the labourer became a decorated garment: this was a typical fashion trend.

The earliest surviving decorated smock is a garment of 1779 from Mayfield in Sussex (now housed in the Victoria and Albert Museum) and recorded as a wedding smock. It is dark coloured and in good condition despite having been handed down through seven generations. An early nineteenth-century example from Wales displays a wealth of stitching: the deep fourteen-inch (36 cm) panel of smocking helps to give the smock its character, which is typical of Wales and the border counties. There is plenty of evidence of regional variations in the size of the smocked panel, often dictated by the type or thickness of the fabric. The two examples illustrated here show the two extremes, but many smocks had panels of moderate size.

The advantage of the technique was that, without drawing elaborate or intricate designs on the fabric beforehand, the grouping and variation of a very few stitches could give a whole series of different rectilinear patterns, and a variety of textures, as the pictures opposite show. The dense

The Mayfield smock of 1779

Evan Griffith's smock from Wales, described above. Can smocking go further?

regular use of the same stitch gives an all-over texture which looks uncannily like plain knitting, as on the Wiltshire smock of 1840. A very different and charming texture is given by a sparse stitching, as shown on the ready-made smock (far right) in which the 'tubes' or gathers are barely held parallel.

Throughout Europe smocking has been practised in bold colours on rich backgrounds. The Italian technique of shirring is closely related to smocking and has had many popular revivals. The shift of Hungarian peasant women often displayed finely smocked fronts. In Spain, Basque peasant women still wear smocked skirts and the young boys smocked blouses, on festive occasions. Thus the smocking technique is not exclusively an English craft, though the application of it to the rural costume, stitched in self-coloured thread, makes the smock-frock an English traditional garment.

Strong twisted linen thread was used singly or doubled in the needle, for both the smocking and the subsequent surface embroidery, and there is a record of an Oxfordshire man early in this

Smock, smocking, smocked

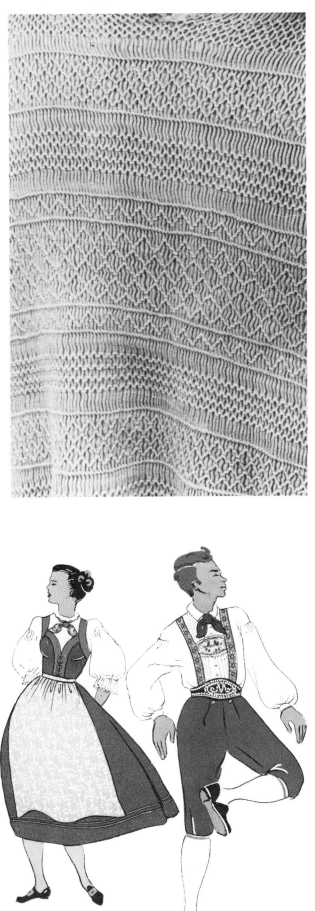

The smocked panel LEFT shows the traditional stitches making a variety of rectilinear patterns. The smock from Wiltshire BELOW shows how cable stitch when closely worked looks like knitting. The ready-made garment BOTTOM although crudely smocked, shows the attractive texture of widely spaced stitching.

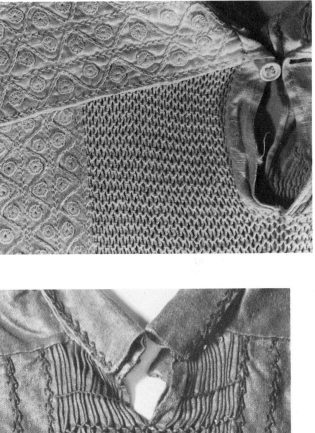

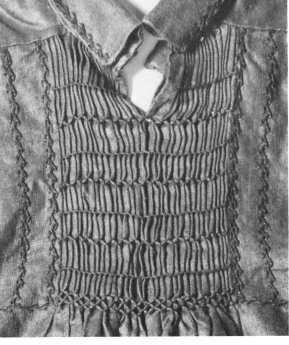

Folk costume from Austria showing gathering related to smocking.

century who as a child waxed the thread in preparation for his mother's task of working the 'crinkle crankle stitch' on the unmade smocks for a local manufacturer.

Counting and picking up at regular intervals the linen threads of the fabric was the method used by the rural housewife for gathering the 'tubes' on her husband's smock-frock. The late nineteenth century brought aids to eliminate the tedium and make the technique less trying on the eyes. These were firstly a template made of perforated card, then the 'iron-on' transfer, marking the fabric with parallel rows of dots, still available and widely used today.

In our own age a gathering machine for home use was designed and popular during the 'do-it-yourself' era of the early sixties, but unfortunately it is only suitable for light-weight fabrics, such as those used in underwear and children's wear. It gathers a depth of 5½ inches (14 cm) and by taking the fabric through a number of times any depth can be gathered. This requires practice but once mastered this little machine eliminates hours of tedious work.

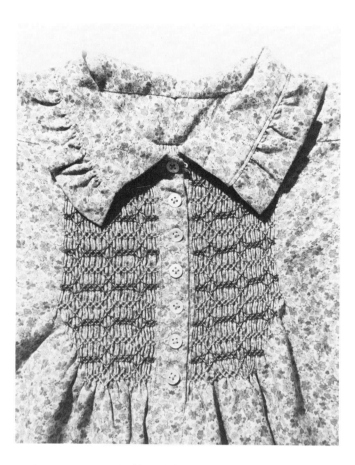

An arrangement of cable and chevron stitches worked in two colours to give a textural effect that complements the print of the fabric.

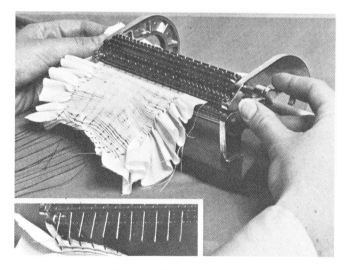

A gathering machine useful for preparing strips of smocking (see suppliers' list).

Modern methods and materials

Smocking can be applied to almost any fabric and worked in an infinite variety of threads. It is relaxing and rhythmical hand work that once mastered is quick to execute. The modern examples illustrated in this book show the craft on fabrics that are popular and easy to obtain. Some materials conveniently lend themselves to the technique as they provide a natural grid for the gathering-threads. These are the ginghams, spotted and regular striped fabrics, which also give interesting visual effects. Traditional fabrics such as linen (holland) or cotton drill with their firmness of weave and creasing properties will form neat 'tubes' more readily than will a loosely woven fabric. Floral Viyella, Tana lawn or any small-patterned fabric such as the Laura Ashley prints, can make beautiful children's dresses, but the stitching needs to be very simple, giving a textural effect which complements rather than distracts from the fabric design. Before buying a patterned fabric, take a look at the underside to ensure that a transferred dot is going to be easily visible.

Even the finest needle can snag the fibres and make ugly linear marks on the surface of a spun or

Smock, smocking, smocked

fine silk, but 'Tussore' or wild silk is naturally textured and can be used for smocking.

Transfers

Smocking dot transfers for ironing on to the fabric are made by Deightons Bros. Ltd (see page 103) and are available in twelve different spacing sizes and in sheets 7 inches (18 cm) deep and 36 inches (91 cm) long. The most versatile sizes are illustrated here, 'K' being the most popular of all. They are printed in silver which shows up light on dark fabrics and dark on light fabrics. Today most transferred markings should wash out — if they do not, they can ruin a delicate piece of work with the shade of the transfer dots apparent even from the right side. It is advisable to confirm this point if using lawn or a similar diaphanous fabric, by transferring a few dots with an iron and washing a sample of the cloth.

The wider spaced the dots, the more fabric will be taken up in the gathers, and the examples illustrated reduce the width of the fabric to approximately one third of its original size. This reduction is affected also by the type of stitches employed and the thickness of the fabric. It is worth experimenting with the chosen fabric and dot spacing to find out exactly how much material will be absorbed for the finished measurement

If the smocking on the garment is to be shaped into a point the transfer can be cut to shape, but make sure that the number of dots in each row is a multiple of four (to make the minimum of two tubes) and that the shape is symmetrical (see below). For your first piece of smocking it is a

Deighton's transfer dots, actual size. Sizes K ABOVE, **and O** BELOW, **for fine fabrics.**

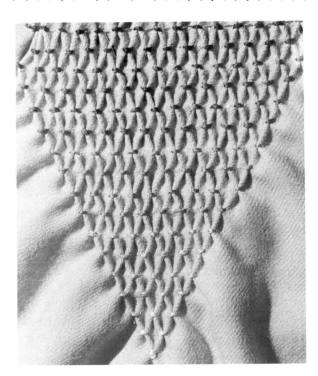

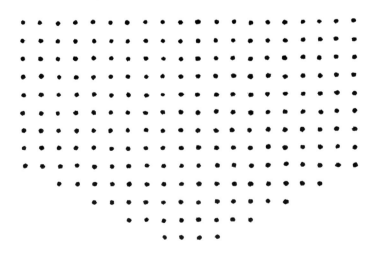

The shallow triangle of dots ABOVE **will give the pointed shape of honeycombing on Viyella** RIGHT, **when gathered.**

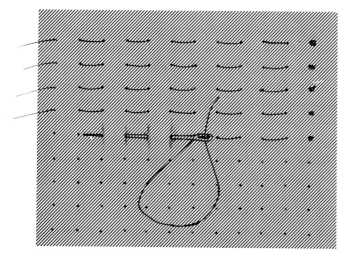

Wrong side of fabric, with transferred dots.

When using needlecord, a transfer is not necessary. Work on the right side of the fabric and gather in multiples of three ribs.

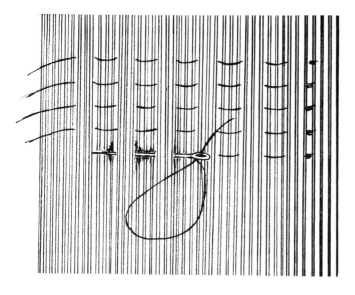

good idea to experiment on a square of cloth similar in texture and weight to the material you will use for the final garment. The transfer maker's name can be cut off the transfer together with surplus rows of dots. Your transfer should have one more row of dots than you intend to sew. Place it down on the wrong side of the fabric, remembering to leave spaces either side for seaming the garment. The straight edge of the transfer placed along the top straight edge of the material should ensure that the rows of dots are parallel with the grain or weave. To check that the grain of the fabric is square, pull out one of the weft threads, to give you a 'straight line' at right angles to the weave.

Pinning or tacking can buckle the transfer, but if a large area is being covered a tacking thread worked along and down the centre to form a cross

is preferable to tacking round the edge. Make sure the transfer is big enough for the area you are going to smock; joining transfers often leads to misplaced dots and difficulty later on. Transfer the dots with a warm iron with positive pressure along the paper and into each corner. Excessive heat will make the dots more difficult to wash out later. Check that every area has made contact by lifting one corner gently before ripping the paper away. You are now ready for the gathering process.

Gathering

Creating the folds of fabric into pipes resembling organ tubes, on which you will play your decorative tune, is simple but repetitive and there is no short cut. It is the care taken at this stage that will ensure a well-embroidered item. Do not use standard tacking thread for this job as it is likely to break when pulling up the gathers. A terylene thread is more suitable as it is stronger, but even this may need to be doubled for heavy linen fabrics. On a pure silk fabric use silk thread. Cut a thread for each line approximately 6 inches (15 cm) longer than the length of material to be gathered and make a large knot at one end. Make the gathering stitches from right to left along each row of dots, inserting the needle into one dot and bringing it out at the next until the row is complete; then leave the thread end loose. Repeat with each row until the area is covered and all the stitches are parallel across the fabric. By this method the dots are concealed between each pleat.

To 'pull up' the work, support the cloth on a large surface, flatten it with the left hand whilst gently pulling pairs of threads with the right hand. Work the fabric up the threads uniformly, rather than pulling at individual threads, which will cause them to break. Stroke down the length of the

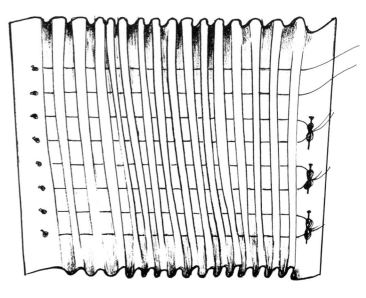

tubes with the eye of a needle as you progress and push them up tightly against each other. Pulling the fabric in the direction of the tubes will help them form and steaming them whilst they are compacted together will help them to retain their shape. Now allow the tubes to distribute themselves evenly to a measurement slightly narrower than the finished work. This allows for the expansion of the embroidered material once the retaining threads have been removed, and the expansion varies with the thickness of the fabric and the type of embroidery stitch.

The tubes should not be too close together: there should be sufficient space between them for the needle to be inserted easily and to allow for the thickness of the embroidery thread. When an even measurement has been achieved trim all the excess thread ends to about 6 inches (15 cm) in length. Secure them by inserting a pin at the end of two rows of threads and twist these round the pin in a figure-of-eight. On fine fabrics it is preferable to use the spare thread to work a couple of back-stitches.

Needles and threads

Twisted threads are the best to use as they are strong and less likely to shred than a stranded variety, thus causing frustration and untidy work. For smocking on clothing it is advisable to use cotton thread on cotton fabrics, silk on silk and linen on linen. This is to avoid alarming distortions when the garment is laundered. Experimental work is not constrained in this way.

Where a traditional textural effect is desired, self-coloured thread or a complementary shade to the fabric is most suitable. Careful choosing of colours is always necessary since too great a variety can distract from the quality and nature of the craft. The modern garments illustrated are each created from the careful combination of fabric, thread and stitches.

DMC and Anchor cotons-à-broder are available in a wide range of colours and thickness. They are the most versatile threads, being suitable for many fabrics and thus ideal for a beginner. They can be used singly or doubled in the needle.

'Lintrad' 16/3 (Henry Campbell's linen smocking thread) is a hard twisted thread in natural colour for use on linen fabric, hessian and for experimental work.

'Lingarn' is a softer linen thread and is available in many colours, single or double twist.

Pearsall's Twisted embroidery silk is limited in its use as it is softly twisted and expensive. A good alternative is Gutermann's silk buttonhole twist, as it is firmly twisted and available in a variety of colours.

Rayon 'Cronit' crochet thread, as used on the maternity dress on page 52, is firmly twisted, shiny and useful for clothing and experimental work.

Always choose a needle suitable for the fabric and with an eye large enough to take the thread without shredding it, but not so large as to leave an ugly hole in the fabric. Needles blunt easily on closely woven linen and cotton, but they can be sharpened and polished on emery paper. (A small 'emery cushion' was used by Victorian needlewomen for this purpose; it was filled with emery powder into which the needles were stabbed two or three times.) The thimble is really useful to protect the end of the finger, and in turn it helps to make smooth speedy stitches. It is very necessary when working on linen and tough cottons.

Designs and stitches

The stitches are divided into two groups: firstly the traditional ones found on the nineteenth century smock-frock, which are variations of 'stem' or 'outline' stitch and give a limited amount of elasticity to the finished work; secondly, chevron and honeycomb stitch, which are later developments of the technique and are employed frequently on children's clothes, as the elasticity of these stitches is far greater than those of the previous group. For this reason care must be exercised when combining the two types in one piece of work. The greater elasticity of the second group may be preferable at the lower edge of the smocking on a child's garment, where, being under continual strain, the stitches are more likely to break.

The smocked panel of the early nineteenth century sample smock from Hereford, which features broad bands of wave and cable stitch, divided by double rows of outline stitch.

Group One: the traditional stitches

The traditional stitches of the smock-frock look their best in self-coloured thread on a plain, checked or striped fabric and worked in alternating broad bands of one type of stitch, positively divided by a single or double row of outline stitch (see above). Do not overcrowd the rows of embroidery as the well-formed tubes have a very pleasing effect unadorned and make a good counterpoint with bands of stitching.

Shepherd's smock in blue linen, with traditional smocking in the front panel. The wavy pattern on collar and shoulders is smocking worked on the underside of the fabric.

Start the embroidery with a knot in the thread carefully hidden in the first tube on the left of the work and back-stitch it down on the wrong side of the fabric. Bring the needle through the first tube to the front of the work and proceed picking up each tube in turn at a regular depth. It is a good rule to start with a row of outline stitch to help organize or 'set' the tubes to lie parallel. Work all the embroidery at an even tension, bearing in mind that the natural tendency is to pull the threads too tight, thus reducing the elasticity of the garment. The retaining threads of the gathers are visible between the tubes and provide a guide for keeping the embroidered lines parallel to each other. Avoid stitching exactly on the line of gathering threads: if they are caught by the needle they will be difficult to remove when the smocking has been completed. Finish off with three or four over-stitches into the last tube on the underside and check that they are very secure, but do not join two tubes together as this will prevent the work from stretching evenly. Also, try to avoid finishing off threads within a line of embroidery, particularly on fine fabrics where the over-stitching will show on the right side. At the same time, it is most important that the initial piece of thread should not be so long that it becomes woolly in appearance towards the end of the row. A convenient length is 12-15 inches (30-38 cm).

Outline stitch is simple and effective. Pick up with the needle a small piece of material on each successive tube and keep the working thread below the needle.

Cable stitch is worked as for outline stitch, but this time the working thread should lie alternately above and below the needle. Make the stitch at right angles to the tube, to keep a neat cable effect.

Wave and trellis stitches are a combination and extension of the previous ones. Using the visible gathering threads to determine the size of the wave or trellis, work upwards keeping the thread below the needle and reverse at the apex of the point so that the thread lies above the needle on the downward movement. This rule applies to all smocking stitches.

Vandyke stitch was found on a few early nineteenth century garments and is the only stitch worked from right to left. Each tube is sewn twice and for this reason it is a very strong stitch, but slow to execute and its zig-zag line makes it the most elastic of the traditional stitches. Bring the needle through to the right side of the work on the second tube and back-stitch the first tube to it with the thread below the needle. Make a back-

Traditional stitches

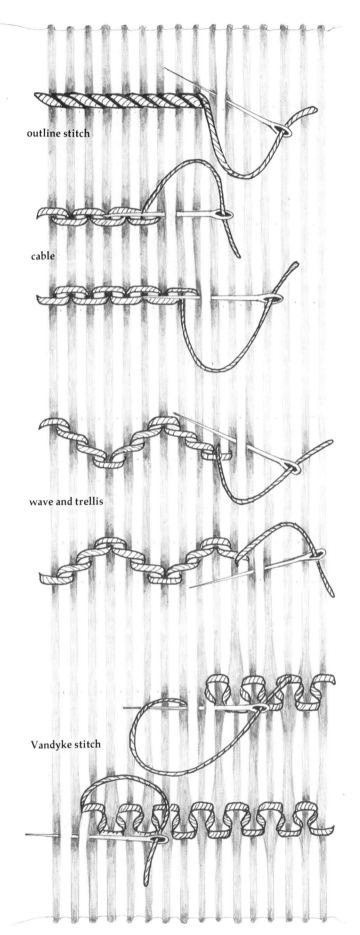

outline stitch

cable

wave and trellis

Vandyke stitch

Smock, smocking, smocked

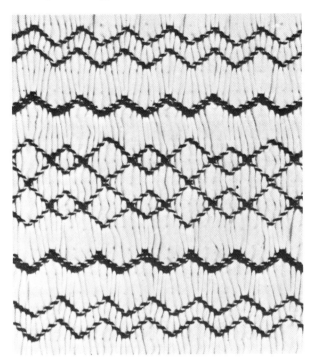

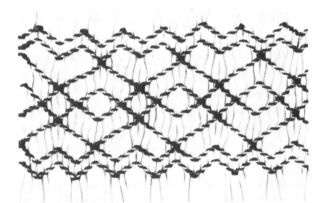

ABOVE and BELOW Wave and trellis stitch varying in size create ideas for interwoven bands of smocking. These designs are particularly suitable for children's wear as they will stretch and have a light weight lace-like quality.

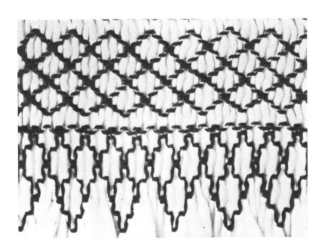

Vandyke stitch is used to create the points on this band of smocking with cabel and trellis stitch above.

49

stitch above into the same tube at the depth required and repeat, alternately above and below, with the threads alternating accordingly.

Group Two: chevron and honeycomb stitches

These more recently developed stitches are less constricting and more stretchy than the traditional stitches. They are less extravagant on the width of the fabric and are quicker to execute. They look most effective in bands or shaped areas and worked in positive colours. They enhance a small print, needlecord, velveteen and many other fabrics for clothing. In experimental work the variety of possible fabrics and combination of threads is unlimited.

Chevron stitch is the most versatile of smocking techniques; it can be varied in depth and width and combined with other stitches. Once mastered it can be very satisfying and is an excellent stitch for children to try. Remembering the rule: thread below the needle when working upwards, and above the needle on the downward movement. Take a back-stitch over two tubes, emerging between them and take the needle up and over the second tube to repeat the back-stitch, alternately above and below. The diagonal stitch joining the back-stitches can be carried over one or two tubes in order to speed up the process. This stitch can be worked in a single row or reversed

A reproduction of a shepherd boy's smock, traditionally embroidered, described with pattern on page 97. The modern needlecord dress for a toddler is smocked with chevron stitch and described, with pattern, on page 100.

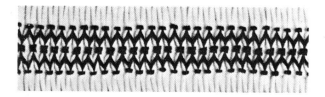

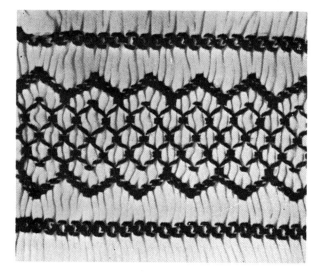

Chevron stitch. When worked on each tube, as in the top drawing, the effect is as above. When worked on alternate tubes, as centre drawing, and reversed as in the bottom drawing, the effect will be as below.

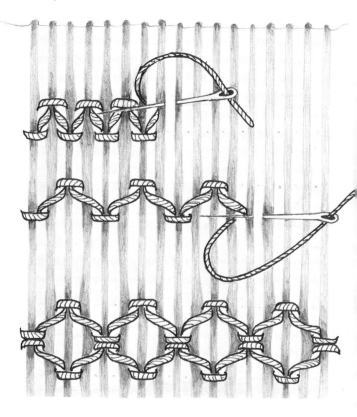

Smock, smocking, smocked

upon itself to form diamonds. Two variations are illustrated below. Firstly, a double-stitched type, secondly, a combination of cable stitch and chevron stitch, as used on the child's floral print party dress. Many more stitches can be invented.

double chevron

chevron and cable

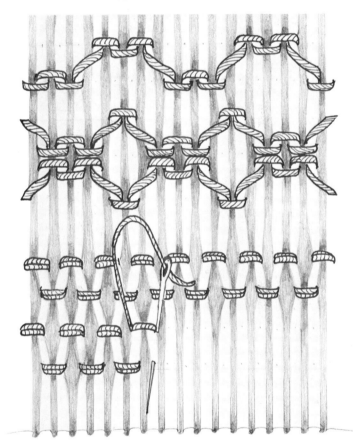

honeycomb

Honeycomb stitch is the quickest method of smocking because two rows are worked simultaneously. It needs some care in execution, and as the majority of the thread is on the underside, it is ideal for patterned or piled fabric where exposed embroidery would be distracting or wasted. Work a double back-stitch over two tubes, then pass the needle down or up through the tube to the position of the next back-stitch. Repeat the movement, alternating up and down along the row, using the gathering-threads as a guide.

The black and white rayon Sarille smock dress is suitable for maternity wear. Mock smocking is worked, using the dots of the fabric, on the front and sleeves, and the back fullness is simply gathered into the yoke. An antique lace collar gives the garment added charm. It is cut to the same system of rectangles as the basic smock on page 76.

Materials required:

approximately 3½ yards of 36 inch rayon sarille
4 pearl buttons
1 reel of rayon Cronit
lace collar
2 sheets of smocking dots size D (unless the fabric is already spotted), cut as follows: 32 inches wide and 7 inches deep for the front, two pieces 17 inches wide and 2½ inches deep for the sleeves.

Follow the pattern on page 76 but omit the collar and cuffs. Mock smock the front to within 2 inches of the selvedge and gather the back between the tailor tacks to fit the yoke. Hem the base of the sleeve and mock smock right across, 2 inches above the hem. Gather the sleeve-head to fit between the tailor tacks of the back and front pieces in step 6. Follow the step-by-step instructions on pages 80-5, omitting steps 4, 5 and 9.

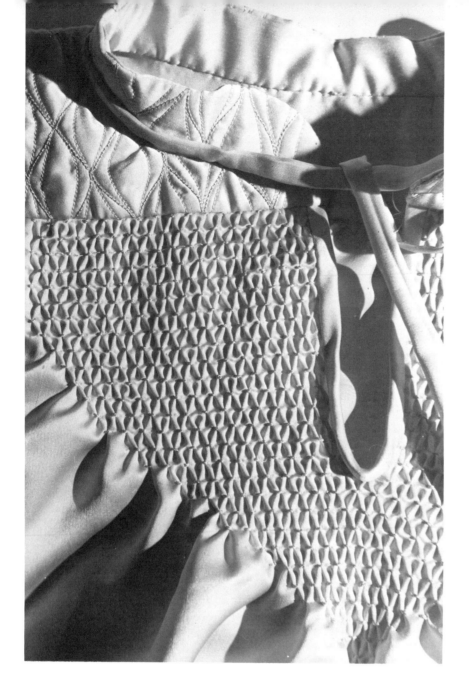

Honeycomb stitch features on a satin blouse with quilted yoke.

Beads, sequins or even tassels can be applied to the smocking when working either chevron or honeycomb stitch.

Finishing

When all the smocking is complete the pins holding the retaining threads can be removed. Whilst flattening the work on a surface with the palm of the left hand, withdraw the threads with the right hand by firmly pulling each knot. If the gathers are to be set into a yoke, the top thread can remain in place with a back-stitch at the required measurement. Gently stretch the smocking and steam press on the underside to improve its appearance.

Honeycomb stitch on hessian decorated with wooden beads.

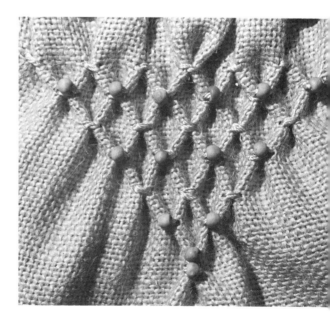

On the smock exhibited at the Great Exhibition, illustrated on page 15, the stitchery on the smocking is used in a figurative way, as leaves, flowers and symbols, and the smocking character merges with embroidery, as shown above.

Smocking as a practical decoration need not be confined to the traditional garment and its variations. Many commercial patterns of children's wear incorporate smocking in the design and provide instructions and transfers. Others can be adapted to take smocked panels by adding the appropriate amount of fabric required in the appropriate area, as on a modern man's shirt front.

Once the principle of smocking is really appreciated it can be applied in a creative way and the basic technique may appear unrecognizable. Interesting clothes can be made with small areas of experimental smocking combined with other embroidery techniques such as quilting or appliqué.

A detail of the modern smocking that appears on the dress on page 87.

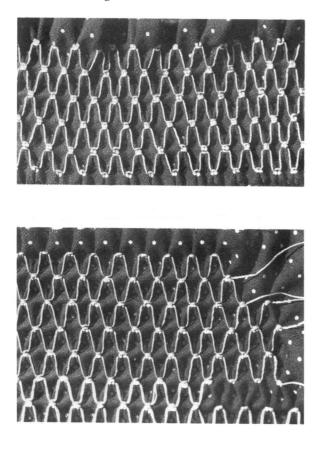

LEFT Samples of Vandyke stitch worked in both the traditional method (upper section) and in mock smocking (lower section).BELOW This wavy pattern appears on the reverse side of mock smocking, and can be used as an alternative texture.

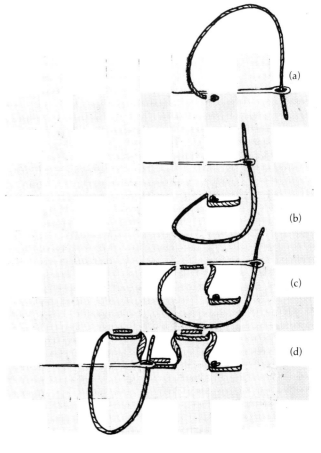

Mock smocking: the arrangement of the threads before pulling up each back-stitch.

Mock smocking

'Mock smocking' is an extension of the craft and looks very like loose examples of the stitches shown in the previous section, but really has nothing in common with them. It does not stretch easily, nor does it require preliminary gathers, and only twice the finished measurement of fabric is needed. It is a useful feature for clothing where a 'smocked' texture is desired on thick fabrics and even knitting.

Care must be exercised when laundering garments that are decorated in this way as the panel does not have the strength or durability of smocking, nor does it retain its shape so readily.

Spotted fabrics or ginghams are the easiest fabrics to use for this method as they provide a grid, but once the technique has been perfected any firmly woven material with size D smocking dots (widely spaced) applied to the right side is suitable. All the stitches of conventional smocking can be worked without preliminary gathers simply by picking up the dots in the same regular system of stitching. This forms a ruched effect rather than the neat parallel pleats of traditional smocking. Some stitches are easier than others and all need practice to perfect a regular tension; Vandyke stitch is the most successful and was used on the rayon maternity dress on page 52. The technique is illustrated in the step by step diagrams.

Wide dots for mock smocking, actual size.

BELOW Honeycomb stitch worked as mock smocking on the right, and in the conventional method on the left.

Mock smocking on a girl's dress of jumbo cord, designed by Sally Tuffin.

Work on the right side of the fabric, from right to left. Pick up the far corner of the first check and make a back-stitch into the near corner of the same check, thus pulling the points together and enclosing the knot in the same movement (a). Work another back-stitch above, picking up first the top right-hand corner then the left-hand corner of the next check and back-stitching them together (b and c). Repeat this process along the fabric, pulling up alternate tops and bottoms of the checks and making sure that the threads which lie between the back-stitches do not pucker the fabric (d). The process is repeated on the next row by picking up the alternate corners to create a honeycomb or diamond effect, as shown left.

This cell-like structure has many possibilities for the decoration of clothing. The embroidered areas can be of varied shape, provided that any transfer used has been cut with an even number of dots in each row. Beads can be applied during or after the ruching process, either in the cell or on the apex of each. Like honeycomb stitch the experimental possibilities of this technique are almost limitless.

57

5 Embroidery

Surface embroidery was a natural development of decoration for the smock, but unlike 'smocking' it has no definite practical purpose. The rectangle of stitchery that flanked the smocked panels of the front and back of the garment became known as the 'box', an area that has provoked much controversy. Many romantic flights of fancy have given a symbolic importance to the embroidery but it is now accepted that the designs were simple expressions of folk art. As on the standing stones of celtic Britain, natural decoration without precedent usually tended towards scrolls, whorls, swags and geometric shapes. The same forms appeared on folk pottery and personal artefacts. In the pre-Roman era the decoration of such items may well have had some mysterious or symbolic role, but we can only make guesses.

Roman and Anglo-Saxon tunics for nobles were decorated at the neckline and wrists with meandering patterns, showing a similarity to the nineteenth century smock-frock in their

Saxon tunics decorated at the neckline, hem and wrists.

An eighth-century bronze relief depicting the crucifixion, from the early Christian civilization in Ireland. It illustrates the characteristic shapes of celtic art.

ornament as well as in their simple style. Many folk costumes of European cultures which are still worn for festive occasions have celtic-type decoration and the Irish dance costume is one such example.

It must not be deduced, however, that there is a continuous tradition of decoration in working clothes. The agricultural smock appeared unadorned during its progress through history, only becoming 'biassed' or 'smocked' in the late eighteenth century. Other than simple lines of stitching on either side of the smocking and around the collar and cuffs, the extended decoration did not appear much before the 1820s. As is often the case with folk decoration, friendly competition resulted in increasing elaboration until the basic design became wildly overdecorated, patterns covering all available surfaces.

Local 'Hirings' gave some purpose to the embellishment. Besmocked workers in search of employment at these fairs give us reason to suppose that the ornate scrolls, leaves, cones etc. had something to do with the wearer's trade. There may have been something in this, but similar designs evolved in some areas regardless of the labourer's occupation, as though an established pattern was inevitably passed from housewife to housewife, each interpreting it individually to suit her skill. Lack of evidence in museums as to the origins of individual smocks makes it impossible to establish any positive theories. In the later stages of smock manufacture

59

Part of the sampler worked by Sarah Bere, who endeavoured to relate the designs to the location and occupation of the wearer of early nineteenth-century smocks.

when cottagers worked the embroidery, one competent 'draughtswoman' may have been responsible for the designs on many garments, whilst another worked the stitchery. The Sunday smock in particular profited from this mode of folk art. Thomas Hardy in *Under the Greenwood Tree* referred to the garments worn by 'stalwart ruddy men and boys as they assembled for the choir; mainly in snow-white smock-frocks, embroidered upon the shoulders and breasts, in ornamental forms of hearts, diamonds and zig-zags.'

The embroidered box was generally found on the round smock and the particularly beautiful ones appear to be dated between 1830 and 1850. The designs ranged from the repetition of the same stitched motif, as on the Wiltshire smock (right) to many other elegant examples with no more than three basic stitches arranged and alternated

The simple floral motifs of this cream linen round smock from Dorset are worked in two varieties of feather stitch.

Small 'eyelets' are interwoven with chain stitch and framed with rows of feather stitch to create a very sophisticated texture on the box, collar and shoulders of the Wiltshire smock, also shown on page 43.

to create complex interlaced designs. Where the larger collars were featured protecting the shoulder areas the embroidery on the yoke was reduced.

Few early smocks were worked in coloured threads but darker-toned or black thread was often employed on the products of the manufacturers of the second half of the century. These garments had sparse designs and comparatively crude stitchery. That the design of later smocks was predetermined, and not improvised, is shown by the blue stencil or ink drawings beneath the embroidery stitches on some existing but unworn examples.

The occupation of the shepherd has produced the most elaborate smocks, with the garment embroidered as a love-token, as well as a useful way of keeping the man warm. On many smocks the embroidery was so heavy that it provided additional weight and added to its value as a

Abstract and figurative designs are worked entirely in single feather stitch in the boxes of the round smock LEFT, and the royal commemorative smock BELOW.

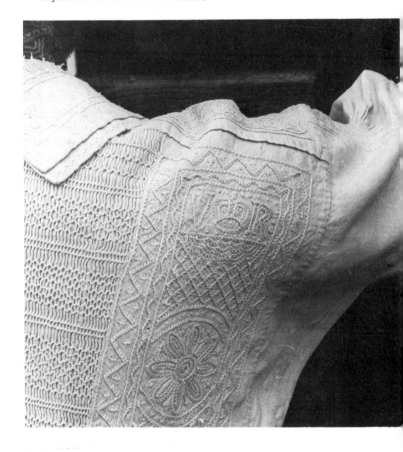

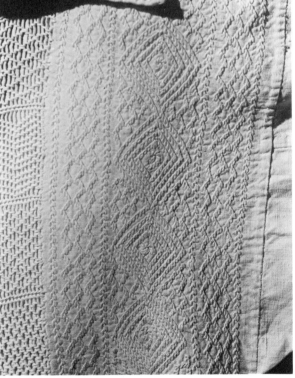

The box of the smock ABOVE displays a variety of feather stitches in double thread. This was a sample garment used by the professional smock maker Mary Bufton of Hereford.

protective garment. The extended epaulettes of the weather-defying garments of the border counties of Wales provided further areas for self expression, and the designs, like those of the traditional quilts, have a strong celtic influence. The whorls, trees and heart-shapes were densely embroidered often in a mirror image design. Some of the smocks had a feather motif incorporated in the design, not unlike the plumes of the Prince of Wales. The celtic swag also appeared on many smocks in single rows either side of the deep

61

Neat herringbone stitch was a feature of the Surrey smocks. These garments, as already mentioned, displayed very little surface decoration; the stitches that were used were functional, to attach the yoke to the garment or to strengthen the edge of the collar. On some of these garments a progression from the simple parallel lines of back-stitch produced wide linear zig-zags and back-stitch was also worked over itself two or three times to form a recurring dot, as seen at the bottom of this page.

Plumes and heart-petalled flowers feature frequently in the embroidery of smocks from South Wales. On this enormous cape LEFT chain stitch, single feather stitch and dot infill are worked in a mirror image design, and treble feather stitch is worked in two rows on the numerous tucks of the outer edge.

smocked panel or repeated in many lines on the tucks of the extended collars and epaulettes. The bold open chain stitches that were employed were closely packed so that little of the background fabric was seen.

The stitches generally used on smocks included single feather stitch (very much like the perennial blanket stitch known to every schoolchild), double and treble feather stitch, known in the nineteenth century as coral-stitch, and a dot technique which provided useful textural filling for small areas.

A selection of designs from Hampshire, Somerset and Herefordshire using feather stitch in swags, wave and zig-zag patterns, with dot infill.

The unusual and exquisite embroidery of a late nineteenth-century child's smock.

The embroiderer has always been held in high esteem and the versatile craft is part of folk tradition. The finer examples of the smock-frock now contribute to this heritage alongside the samplers, chemises, and other embroideries of the Victorian housewife. Embroidery played an important part in the lives of most nineteenth century women; the middle class housewife developed the art as a social grace and those of the less-privileged social groups plied their needles up to twenty hours a day to earn a living.

With the advent of the embroidery transfer around 1900 folk embroidery became a commercialized vogue. Embroidery can be applied to almost any material, as the design is not determined by the weave of the fabric, and colourful free stitchery featured in abundance.

Attempts to revive the simple stitchery and the complex designs of the smock-frock appeared in the professional embroidery magazines in the mid 1920s and again in the late 1950s. In England Olivia Pass, who saw the beauty of the surface decoration of the traditional smock-frocks of a hundred years before, did much to popularize the form. She adapted and applied the shapes and stitches to meet the demands and trends of that time: colourful work on dark backgrounds that enhance the stitchery.

The simple stitches

The effect of the densely embroidered areas on some smocks may appear daunting, but on close examination it is apparent that the three or four stitches employed are amongst the first learnt in any needlework class. No expert skills are required, only the wish to create something individual.

The designs provided below can be interpreted and modified to suit many tastes and abilities, from the single line of feather stitch giving a neat finishing effect to the collar and smocked panels, to the highly ornate motifs on the box. The surface stitching that had a functional purpose could be similarly used today, either to strengthen a weak join in the garment, or to attach a patch pocket or shoulder piece. In these instances use back-stitch or herringbone: the latter provides double strength by the two rows of back-stitch worked in unison.

The stitches illustrated are all closely related to one another and once the parent stitch has been mastered the others are natural developments. The threads I recommend for the surface embroidery are the same as those suggested for the smocking. The self-coloured effect is continued for the traditional smock, but experiment can show the possibilities of coloured threads.

63

Embroidery

Chain stitch Bring the thread out at the top of the line to be embroidered and hold it down on the material with the left thumb. The needle is then inserted into the exact spot where the thread first emerged and is brought out again over the working thread a short distance along, according to the size of stitch required. Repeat the process making sure that the stitches are of equal length and that the threads are not pulled tightly, as this would make the links oval instead of round.

Open chain stitch looks very similar to the previous stitch but is broader and more effective when covering a large area with ever-decreasing shapes or circles, as on many of the collars and epaulettes of traditional garments. Work as for chain stitch, but insert the needle at an angle to the right side of the point where the thread emerges, and make a short squat stitch. The loop formed must be left slack to help create the broad effect.

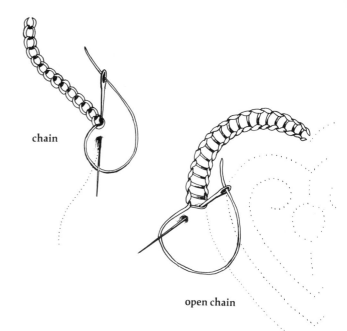

chain

open chain

Single feather stitch is similar to blanket stitch except that the 'arms' of the stitch lie at an angle to the line of the work. The movement of the needle and hand are the same as for chain stitch. Bring the needle through on the line to be worked and insert it in a slanting direction from the right, emerging on the line and over the working thread. Repeat, keeping the stitches an even length and the 'arms' at the same angle. This stitch was used more often than any other, both for a linear effect and for the curves of whorls, teardrops and heart motifs. A variation was effectively used on the unusual smock from Wiltshire (page 60) where the stitching technique was very similar, but the arms met in the centre of an anti-clockwise circle, thus making a small 'eyelet' and giving the work a lace-like quality. The 'eyelet' motif has potentially many variations of size and arrangement for present day smocks.

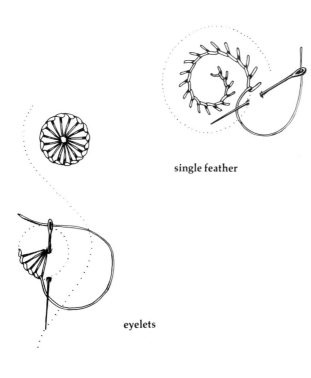

single feather

eyelets

treble feather

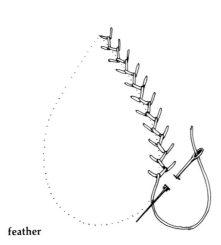

feather

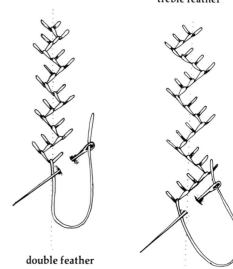

double feather

64

A selection of embroidery patterns, two thirds actual size, LEFT in feather and single feather stitches, CENTRE in feather stitch, chain stitch and eyelets, and RIGHT in feather stitch with chain stitch for the florets.

Feather stitch was frequently used to border the embroidered box, in parallel rows or worked within the design itself. It is only suitable for gentle flowing curves, or for softening hard straight lines. Work as for single feather stitch, creating the 'arms' either side of a centre line, by laying the thread at an angle and stitching alternately from the left and right.

Double and treble feather stitches are extensions of the previous type and were employed on smocks from emany areas. They create zig-zags of various sizes according to the number of arms on each branch of the stitch. Work as for feather stitch with two more 'arms' to the right; turn the work with the

thread lying at right-angles and the needle inserted parallel to the previous branch, work the same number of 'arms' on the left. Then repeat, making the same angle for each branch.

A selection of traditional designs

A variety of the embroidery designs of the garments illustrated throughout the book are drawn in reduced size above and on the following pages. They can be used as they are or in sections for different parts of the smock. All surface embroidery should be worked before making the garment and in the case of collars, cuffs and yoke, only the top surface is embroidered.

Four box designs ABOVE in feather stitches, and two collar designs BELOW in open chain and feather stitch.

Box pattern from a wedding smock from Sussex, illustrated on page 13.

Transfers

Some suitable designs are available as 'iron-on' transfers, but are limited to the familiar pine cone motif with scrolls and parallel lines. Transferring the embroidery design from a drawing to the fabric can be a hazardous task. Ordinary typist's carbon paper is messy and should be avoided. Dressmaker's carbon, which is available in several colours, is a better quality and when used carefully is the most successful method for most types of fabric. Trace the design from the page with grease-proof or similar paper. To transfer the image to the fabric, redraw from top

A modern coat smock with eyelets and pine-cone motif embroidery. For pattern, see page 79.

to bottom to avoid smudging, with the carbon face down between the grease-proof and the right side of the fabric. Follow the maker's instructions and to avoid heavy carbon lines on a fine fabric use a small 'tracing wheel' rather than a pencil to give a tiny dotted image, and on the very tight curves dot the line with a finely pointed instrument.

An 'embroidery transfer pencil' will make an instant home-made transfer by tracing the design on to grease-proof paper. It is only available in blue, and only suitable for cotton or linen fabrics. Keep the pencil sharp to produce a fine line or a series of dots which will be covered by the embroidery stitches. Treat as a conventional transfer and iron the image on to the fabric with a warm iron. The temperature of the iron must be only just sufficient to transfer the design to the fabric, so that the blue marks will subsequently wash out easily. It is good practice to transfer the same areas of the design on to each half of the garment alternately and to ensure symmetry remember to reverse the design for left and right sides. This will mean retracing the design through the grease-proof paper to make the transfer double sided.

The finished embroidery should be steam pressed on the under-side and the pieces are then ready to be assembled.

The embroidery design from the epaulette of a child's garment. Open chain stitch gives this design its dense effect, enhanced by feather stitch.

A linen coat smock makes a practical overgarment for outdoor play. Follow the instructions for the shepherd boy's smock, on page 96-8.

'That smocks should become extinct is greatly to be regretted for they are practical and beautiful garments which would still serve a very useful as well as decorative purpose', wrote Alice Armes in 1926. A sentiment which I share.

Unfortunately present day life styles give us no justifiable reason for producing an entirely hand-made garment, other than for personal satisfaction. The domestic sewing maching is a blessing to every household. As much functional sewing as possible should be carried out by machine, leaving time and energy to perfect and enjoy the hand work, which should embellish the garment in a unique and individual way. Just as in 1880, trend-setters saw the value of the smock as being both practical and stylish, so today spinners, weavers, sculptors, potters and many young people who wish to reflect a new and long lasting fashion are wearing the undateable smock.

The examples of the smock illustrated in colour on pages 34, 51, 52, 70 and 88 are suggestions for styles to suit modern active life. They are simple to cut and assemble and are imaginatively decorated. The fundamental sewing processes are clearly illustrated, showing professional short-cuts and methods that make dressmaking enjoyable. The choice of styles, fabrics and smocking techniques makes for a variety of garments, and a unique way of expressing personal taste in clothes. The entirely reversible smock with all its pieces cut from rectangles, which had many advantages in the Victorian era, is in fact not a comfortable garment to wear, so

6
Making a smock for today

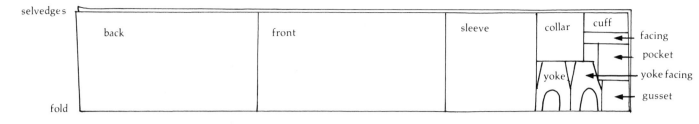

the shoulder yokes of these smocks are shaped like those of the Welsh border garments.

The method of cutting is the result of observing and measuring many nineteenth century smock-frocks and adapting the plan'to present day needs and fabrics. The 'lay' or method of cutting is exactly like the historical garment, where the majority of seams are on the straight grain or parallel to the selvedge, thus enabling the maker to utilize the unfraying edge to her advantage and make maximum use of the fabric.

The heavy cotton smocks (pages 34 and 88) and the shepherd's linen coat smock (pages 33 and 69) are described as outer garments, functional and warm. The black and white rayon Sarille smock-dress (page 52) is suggested for maternity wear, and is decorated with mock smocking and an antique lace collar. The silk evening dress (page 87) and blouse (opposite) are far removed from the original nineteenth-century garment but are still simply cut on the basis of rectangles. The only pattern required is that of the yoke as all the garments hang from the shoulder.

The cutting instructions for the smocks illustrated are provided on nearby pages, and are in three sizes according to the chest or bust measurement: small (34-36 inches, 86-91 cm), medium (38-40 inches, 97-102 cm), and for men, large (42-44 inches, 107-112 cm). No expert fitting skills are necessary and a simple speedy method of construction eliminates the need for temporary tacking of seams in most instances. Basic sewing equipment will suffice but a swing-needle sewing machine for a zig-zag stitch will assist with the finishing of seams and with buttonholes. A steam iron is better than an ordinary iron when working on pure linen and 100 per cent cotton fabrics.

As the majority of the seams are straight, even an inexperienced needlewoman will have no difficulty making up the garment, but should choose an inexpensive easy-to-handle fabric such as cotton drill, calico or gingham. The measurement from the back of the neck down to the required length multiplied by three will determine the amount of fabric required of a 36 inches (91 cm) or 40 inches (102 cm) wide cloth. If the garment is to be full length twice the

measurement from neck to hem plus approximately one yard (91 cm) for sleeves and trims should be sufficient. These estimations are intended only as a guide and excess fabric can be utilized for pockets, trial samples etc.

Suitable fabrics

Cotton drill, gingham, calico, cotton ticking and light-weight denims are all practical to work with and to wear. They are inexpensive and easily obtainable but unless they are guaranteed pre-shrunk, they should be washed before cutting: 100 per cent cottons and pure linen can shrink considerably. To test a fabric for shrinkage cut two pieces identical and generous in size and match them after laundering only one piece, note the difference in size and consider that $\frac{1}{4}$ inch shrinkage on a 9 inch square is equal to 1 inch per yard, or about 3 per cent.

Linen can be difficult to obtain and is comparatively expensive, but a good quality linen twill or Dowlas are both cool to handle and their weight gives excellent draping qualities to a garment. Linen is very hard wearing and for a genuine facsimile it is preferable despite the disadvantage of creasing easily.

Needlecord and other napped fabrics will not shrink, and require no extra length, but great care will be needed after cutting the pieces: chalk an arrow on the reverse side of each piece in the direction of the pile or pattern to ensure that each section is the right way up during the making process. The delicate fibres of lawn and pure silk demand special care with equipment and handling to prevent them from snagging and thus spoiling the surface of the fabric.

The needle of the sewing machine must be sharp and fine — 60 or 70 for European makes and 8 or 10 for English and American sewing machines. A fine ball-point needle is equally suitable. Hand sewing needles must be fine and pure silk sewing thread is necessary both for sewing by hand and machine.

Attractive modern interpretations of the smock can be made in many of the rayon, polyester and rayon blends, Viyella, other medium weight

The silk evening dress and blouse are far removed from the original nineteenth-century garment but serve as illustrations of the smock style applied to modern fashions and fabrics. The effective overblouse features quilted yoke, honeycomb smocking and a simple mandarin collar finished with the rouleau tie. The full-length smock is made of tussore silk and is embroidered with appliqué and random smocking. The back fullness is simply pleated into the yoke and the neckline is finished with a small stand-up shirt collar.

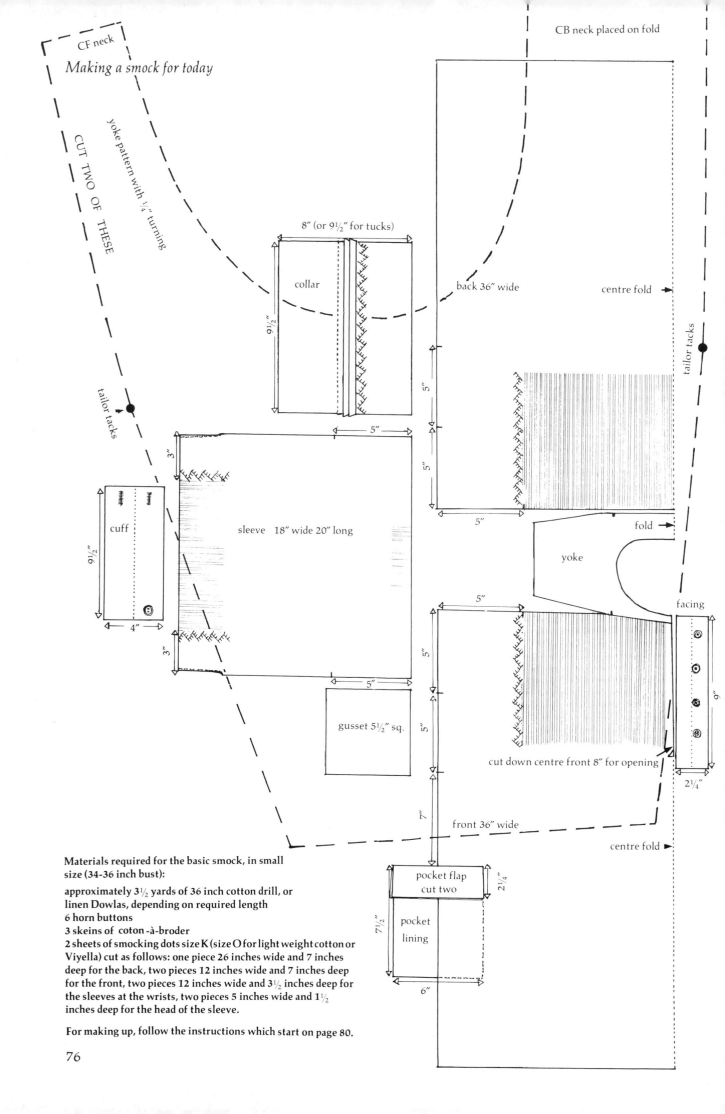

CF neck

Making a smock for today

yoke pattern with ¼″ turning

CUT TWO OF THESE

tailor tacks

CB neck placed on fold

8″ (or 9½″ for tucks)

collar

9½″

back 36″ wide

centre fold

tailor tacks

3″

5″

sleeve   18″ wide 20″ long

5″

5″

5″

fold

cuff

9½″

4″

yoke

facing

3″

5″

5″

5″

9″

gusset 5½″ sq.

cut down centre front 8″ for opening

2¼″

7″

front 36″ wide

centre fold

pocket flap
cut two

2¼″

7½″

pocket
lining

6″

**Materials required for the basic smock, in small
size (34-36 inch bust):**

approximately 3½ yards of 36 inch cotton drill, or
linen Dowlas, depending on required length
6 horn buttons
3 skeins of coton-à-broder
2 sheets of smocking dots size K (size O for light weight cotton or
Viyella) cut as follows: one piece 26 inches wide and 7 inches
deep for the back, two pieces 12 inches wide and 7 inches deep
for the front, two pieces 12 inches wide and 3½ inches deep for
the sleeves at the wrists, two pieces 5 inches wide and 1½
inches deep for the head of the sleeve.

For making up, follow the instructions which start on page 80.

76

closely-woven fabrics and light-weight wool flannel. Synthetic diaphanous materials such as polyester crepe or Dicel satin, if handled by an experienced dressmaker, will make luxurious smock-type garments for evening wear.

Laundering a smock is no problem; the cotton and linen garments can be machine washed and even boiled, but subsequent steam or damp pressing will be necessary. Other more delicate materials should be washed according to the nature of the fabric. Pull the smocking whilst wet in the direction of the tubes to help retain its shape and elasticity.

Key steps in making a smock

1 Cut
2 Smock
3 Embroider
4 Make up

Cutting and preparation

Before cutting endeavour to create a straight edge across the fabric at right-angles to the selvedge by pulling a thread of the weft, then fold and press the cloth lengthwise with the wrong side uppermost. A large flat surface is esssential for cutting; chalk out the pieces and cut with large scissors along a single thread of the fabric if possible. The cutting illustrations are for the small, medium and large smock in the three most authentic styles. They serve to show the measurements of each piece and the matching-up points within each rectangle which are essential for the making up process. Mark these and the centre back (cb) neck of the yoke with a tailor tack, and as all the smaller pieces of the garment are a similar size, chalk an identification mark on each. There is approximately ⅜ inch (1 cm) seam allowance on all seams unless stated otherwise in the instructions; any more than this creates tedious trimming off of surplus fabric during the making up process. No additional interfacings or stiffenings are used; the large flat collars can be

tucked, which will decorate and serve the function of weighting and stiffening the outer edges.

Remember when cutting to allow approximately ¾ inch (2 cm) more fabric on the depth of the collar for each additional tuck.

Make as much use of the selvedges as possible; the neck edge of the collar is placed along the selvedge as this will help reduce the bulk of the fabric in that area when the garment is constructed, and this also applies to the cuff. Where a selvedge does not occur, zig-zag or neaten the edges before smocking and embroidering as they will fray from excessive handling. Stay-stitching on a single layer around the curve of the neck on the yoke will help to retain its shape.

The material has been cut and prepared. Now is the time to smock and embroider the pieces of fabric. Smocking is an integral part of the garment rather than added embellishment. It is carried out now after cutting and preparing the pieces and before sewing them together. The embroidery should be carried out after the smocking.

Make up

When machining, a stable surface with ample space on your left to support the work is essential. Likewise when pinning, folding and pressing, the material should be easily accessible, well lit and supported. Here, the added height of a sleeve board prevents stooping and helps with the more difficult pressing processes.

The *Workwoman's Guide* of 1840 claimed on the front page that 'method shortens labour', and successful dressmaking today relies on a well-organized system of construction and the right choice of sewing methods to suit the fabric and individual maker. As in the nineteenth century the housewife adapted the instructions or suggestions for smock making to suit her skill, so today these step-by-step instructions are only intended as a guide, but have been used on many present day smocks.

When joining two pieces together, pinning prior to machining will suffice in most instances, but for the inexperienced machinist tacking is advisable. When machining, arrange the bulk of the garment to the left of the machine so that only the area being sewn is under the machine 'arm'. Reverse a few stitches at the beginning and end of each seam to prevent them from pulling undone and then trim off the cotton ends. Use small sharp scissors to layer the turnings where possible, thus reducing bulkiness in the collar, yoke and cuffs.

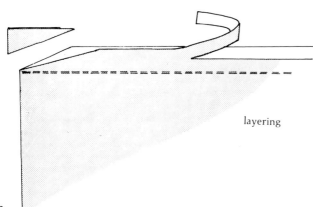

layering

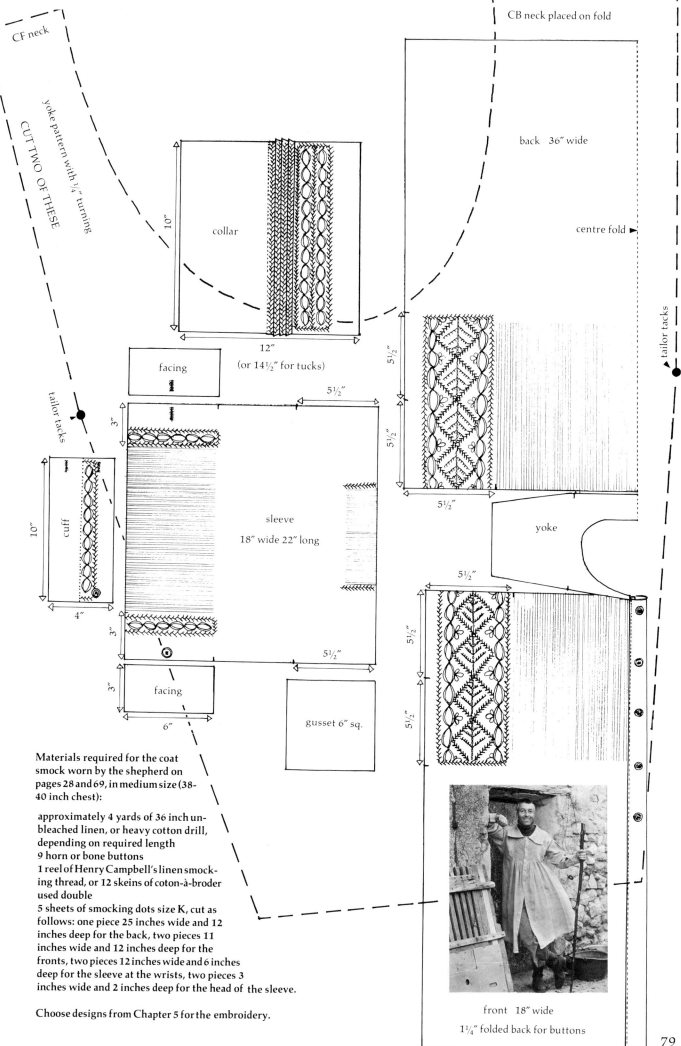

CF neck

yoke pattern with ¼" turning

CUT TWO OF THESE

collar

10"

12"
(or 14½" for tucks)

facing

3"

tailor tacks

cuff

10"

4"

3"

facing

6"

sleeve
18" wide 22" long

5½"

5½"

gusset 6" sq.

back   36" wide

centre fold ▶

tailor tacks ◀

5½"

5½"

5½"

yoke

5½"

5½"

5½"

Materials required for the coat smock worn by the shepherd on pages 28 and 69, in medium size (38-40 inch chest):

approximately 4 yards of 36 inch un-bleached linen, or heavy cotton drill, depending on required length
9 horn or bone buttons
1 reel of Henry Campbell's linen smocking thread, or 12 skeins of coton-à-broder used double
5 sheets of smocking dots size K, cut as follows: one piece 25 inches wide and 12 inches deep for the back, two pieces 11 inches wide and 12 inches deep for the fronts, two pieces 12 inches wide and 6 inches deep for the sleeve at the wrists, two pieces 3 inches wide and 2 inches deep for the head of the sleeve.

Choose designs from Chapter 5 for the embroidery.

front   18" wide
1¼" folded back for buttons

79

Making a smock for today

Good pressing is as important as good machining; always press each seam as it is sewn. This not only helps with the next process of construction, but also ensures that your garment will have a well finished appearance.

Twelve easy steps to make a smock

Note: on all the drawings illustrating these stages, the shaded areas indicate the inside of the fabric or garment.

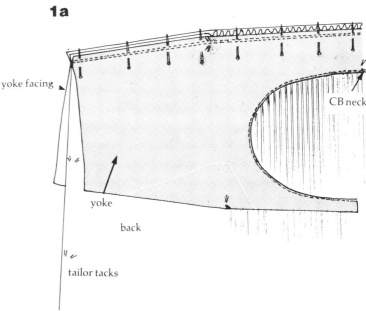

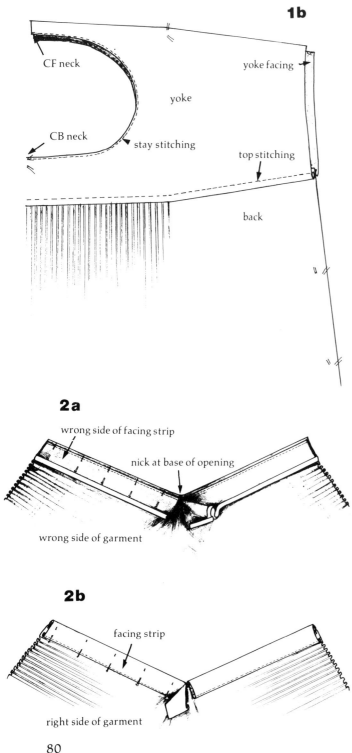

1 *Attaching the yoke*

(a) Join the yoke to the back of the garment with the right sides together, matching the tailor tacks either side of the smockinghe, tack and machine. Repeat the process with the yoke facing joined to the underside of the garment and machine slightly above the previous row. If the turnings are bulky, layer them by trimming the yokes slightly lower than the garment and press both yokes upwards.
(b) A row of top-stitching will help to make this a firm strong seam.

2 *Facing out the front opening*

(a) Cut the facing strip for the underside of the opening 1 inch (2.5 cm) shorter than the other and press ¼ inch (6 mm) fold along one edge of both strips and at the base of the longer one. Place the unfolded edges of the strips to the wrong side of the garment on the centre front opening. Pin, tack and machine them closely to the edges; they should be parallel at the top of the garment, the short strip ending exactly at the base of the slit and the longer one extending a further 1 inch (2.5 cm) and left unstitched.

(b) Nick the turnings at the base of the opening to enable you to press open the narrow seams. Fold each facing strip over to the right side of the garment so their pressed ¼ inch (6 mm) turnings meet the smocking either side of the opening, then press firmly. Sew down the strips by hand or machine, leaving the extra 1 inch (2.5 cm) of the longer strip unstitched.

80

2c

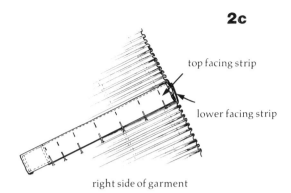

top facing strip

lower facing strip

right side of garment

(c) Place the longer strip over its short partner, lining up the rows of smocking perfectly and pin in position. The overlapping inch (2.5 cm) at the base of the opening should lie flat over the raw edge of the lower strip. Make sure all its raw edges are turned under and press, pin, then tack it down before stitching firmly in a square, ensuring that the lower strip is well secured at the base of the opening.

3a

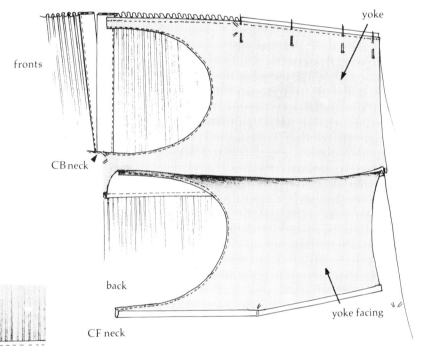

yoke

fronts

CB neck

back

CF neck

yoke facing

3b

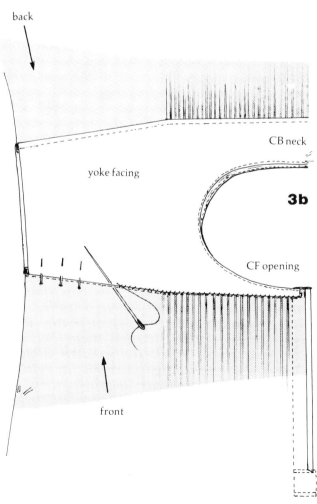

back

yoke facing

CB neck

CF opening

front

3 *Attaching the fronts to the yoke*

(a) With the right sides of the fabric together, join the yokes to the fronts, matching the tailor tacks either side of the smocking. Machine, thus securing the width of the smocking at the top of the front, then layer the turnings and press the yokes upwards.

(b) Press approximately a ¼ inch (6 mm) fold along the edge of the yoke facing and sew by hand or machine to the stitching of the previous join on the inside of the garment, encasing all raw edges of the smocking.

4 *Making the collar*

Fold each collar piece with the right side of the
fabric inside and the selvedge ⅜ inch (1 cm) below
the cut edge. If tucks are required they should be
worked first, along the outer edge of the upper
half. Machine the sides together ¼ inch (6 mm) in
from the edge, trim off the corners of the turnings
and layer if necessary. Turn the collar through to
the right sides and press. When working on a pair
of pieces as on the collars, cuffs, pockets etc.,
always work them in unison, checking that they
are identically matched in size and shape and that
you have right and left partners.

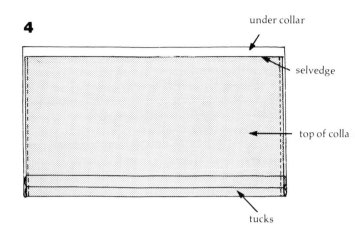

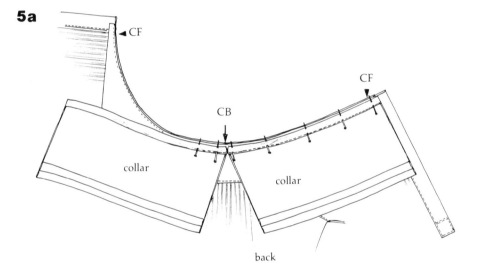

5 *Attaching the collar to the smock*

(a) Pin the projecting underside of the collar to the
right side of the garment through both layers of
the yoke. Start at the centre back and ease the
curved neck edge of the yoke on to the straight
edge of the collar. Work all round to the centre
front seam of the garment and facing strip. Tack
and machine carefully, reversing two or three
times at the centre-back where the two collars
meet.

(b) Layer the turnings generously and cut out V
shapes at the centre-back and front, similarly all
round at regular intervals as close to the machine-
stitch as possible.

(c) Press the turnings up into the collar and bring
the selvedge over all the raw edges of the
yoke and front smocking. Sew it firmly just above
the machine stitching. Work a few strong over-
stitches at the centre-back joining the two collars
together. The remaining centre-front facing
which protrudes beyond the collar should now be
trimmed, turned inside itself and neatly oversewn.

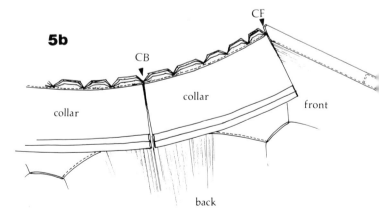

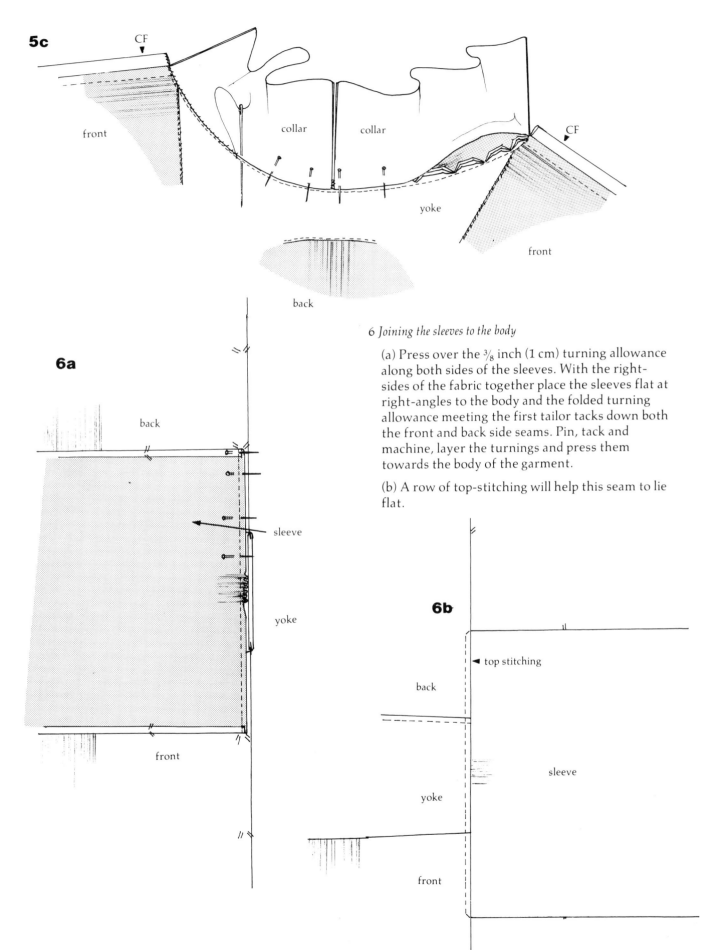

5c

front

CF

collar

collar

yoke

front

CF

back

6a

back

sleeve

yoke

front

6 Joining the sleeves to the body

(a) Press over the ⅜ inch (1 cm) turning allowance along both sides of the sleeves. With the right-sides of the fabric together place the sleeves flat at right-angles to the body and the folded turning allowance meeting the first tailor tacks down both the front and back side seams. Pin, tack and machine, layer the turnings and press them towards the body of the garment.

(b) A row of top-stitching will help this seam to lie flat.

6b

back

◄ top stitching

sleeve

yoke

front

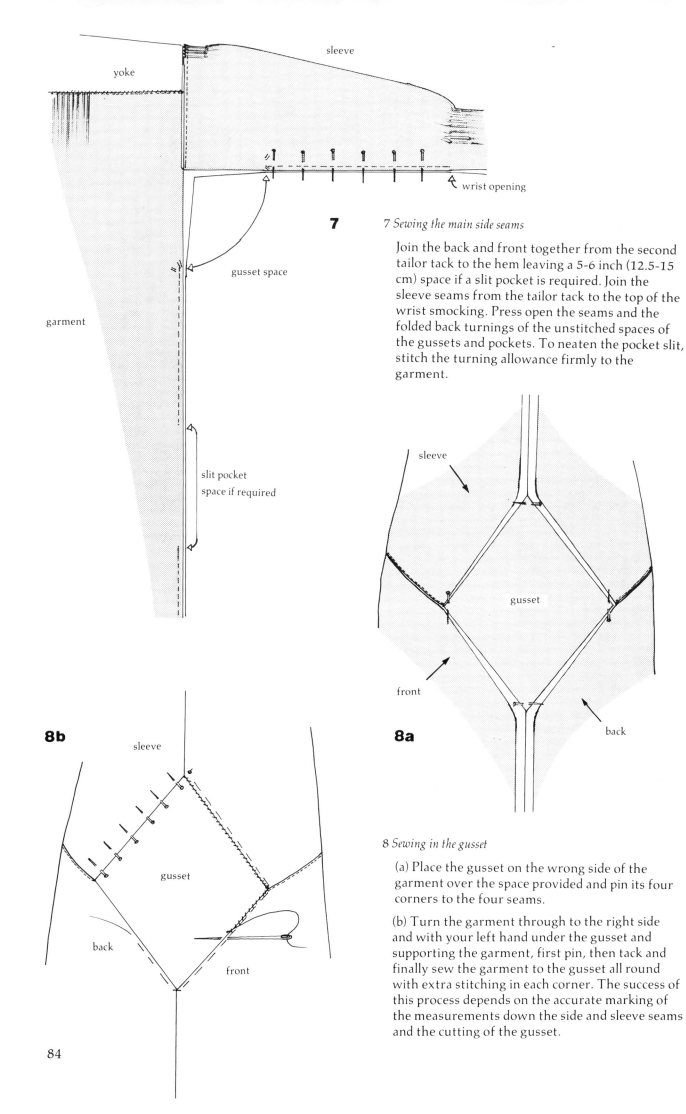

7

sleeve

yoke

garment

gusset space

slit pocket space if required

wrist opening

7 Sewing the main side seams

Join the back and front together from the second tailor tack to the hem leaving a 5-6 inch (12.5-15 cm) space if a slit pocket is required. Join the sleeve seams from the tailor tack to the top of the wrist smocking. Press open the seams and the folded back turnings of the unstitched spaces of the gussets and pockets. To neaten the pocket slit, stitch the turning allowance firmly to the garment.

sleeve

gusset

front

back

8a

8b

sleeve

gusset

back

front

8 Sewing in the gusset

(a) Place the gusset on the wrong side of the garment over the space provided and pin its four corners to the four seams.

(b) Turn the garment through to the right side and with your left hand under the gusset and supporting the garment, first pin, then tack and finally sew the garment to the gusset all round with extra stitching in each corner. The success of this process depends on the accurate marking of the measurements down the side and sleeve seams and the cutting of the gusset.

84

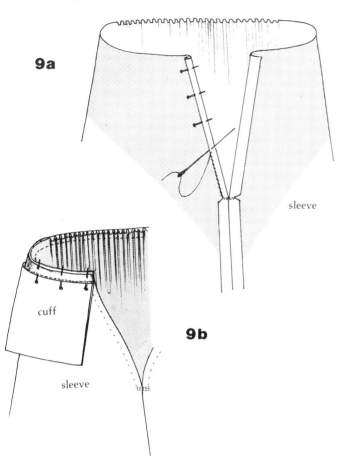

9a

cuff

sleeve

9b

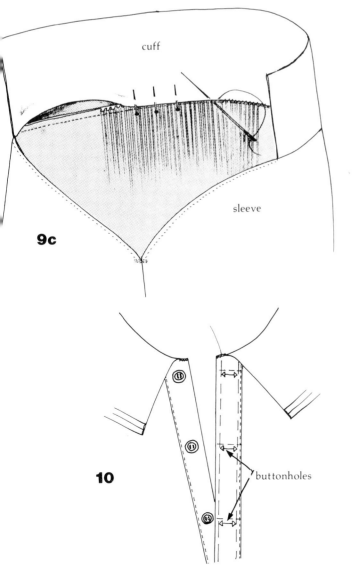

cuff

sleeve

9c

10

buttonholes

9 *Finishing off the ends of the sleeves*

(a) On the inside of the wrist opening make and sew a small hem with the turning allowance. Sew very firmly across the base of the opening by hand or machine.

(b) Make and attach the cuffs in a similar manner to the collar, perfectly lining up the sides of the cuff with the hemmed opening, then machine, trim and press the turnings into the cuff.

(c) Bring over the selvedge to encase the raw edges and sew firmly by hand or machine.

10 *The buttons and buttonholes*

Sew the required number of buttons equally spaced down the centre-front facing and one on the front side of each cuff. Make a good 'shank' to prevent undue stress on the fabric and stitches. Mark the buttonholes carefully with parallel lines of tacking, 1/8 inch (3 mm) wider than the diameter of the button and at right-angles to the edge of the facing. Work them by hand or machine.

11 *Turning the hem*

Trim the fabric level if necessary and turn up a small hem to make the garment the required length. Press it before sewing by hand or machine.

12 *Making the pockets*

The slit in the side seam, as on many early nineteenth century garments, gives access to trouser pockets; or a large patch sewn over the slit on the underside of the garment makes a complete pocket. A patch-pocket can be attached decoratively or the more experienced dressmaker could make the flapped poacher's pocket.

Buttons

A well made smock needs the added authenticity of antique buttons. Everyday buttons of the nineteenth century are not difficult to find; many market stalls and bric-a-brac shops have them either carded or strung together for convenience, or simply cut from disintegrated garments and stored in a button box. It is worth searching through these containers to find five or six matching buttons. Late eighteenth and early nineteenth century smocks had brass buttons with soldered shanks and many later garments had metal buttons with countersunk holes to prevent the stitching from wearing out, with the maker's name inscribed around the rim. These buttons were almost indestructible and many can still be found.

Bone buttons, polished or unpolished, featured as frequently as the previous type. Some are still available, but finding a number that have worn evenly is difficult. The vegetable ivory button (from the kernel of the corozo or dum nut) replaced the bone button in the second half of the nineteenth century, but by then the smock as a countryman's garment was already declining, so these buttons were generally only used to replace the original ones. They were produced in large quantities, but few have survived. Dorset thread or wheel buttons give an excellent finishing touch to hand embroidered garments. They were found on only late nineteenth century smocks, which were possibly revival garments, where the maker had taken advantage of the opportunity also to revive the art of the hand-made thread button. Mass-produced linen-covered buttons for underwear had caused the local thread button industries to decline and cards of linen-covered buttons are still available, their quaint close 'eyes' making them an attractive feature for children's smocks.

Horn buttons were found on many English smock-frocks. They are still made by James Grove and Sons in Halesowen near Birmingham. Modern horn buttons are a good choice as they give an uncluttered natural finish. Mollusc shell buttons, often mistaken for mother-of-pearl (they are thicker and have a milky white appearance), were used frequently on the smock-frock, and many elegant varieties of genuine mother-of-pearl were found on the 'Surrey' and children's smocks. Both these types of pearl button were mass-produced and imported and some are still available. Small early glass buttons, or 'Austrian tinies', will enhance the silk and rayon adaptations of the smock. When buying old buttons purchase one or two extra, if possible, as you will never be able to match them again.

RIGHT The ultimate in smock revivals, dateless and refreshing. The smocking is imaginatively worked in random outline stitch to represent tree-bark. The birds and leaves are appliquéd lightly to the garment and the total effect is finished with tiny dome buttons covered in the two shades of the silk fabric used in the garment. See page 75.

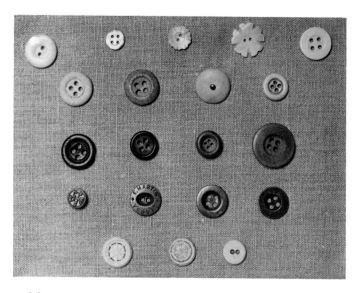

Buttons for a present day interpretation. The top row displays a variety of pearl buttons. The second row features bone buttons with a polished example on the right. The left-hand pair of the centre row is horn; the smaller one is a modern variety and the others are possibly vegetable ivory. The metal buttons of the fourth row are, from left to right, an 'Austrian tiny' and three brass buttons with countersunk holes. The bottom row features a modern 'Dorset Wheel' with an original nineteenth-century example and the perennial linen-covered button.

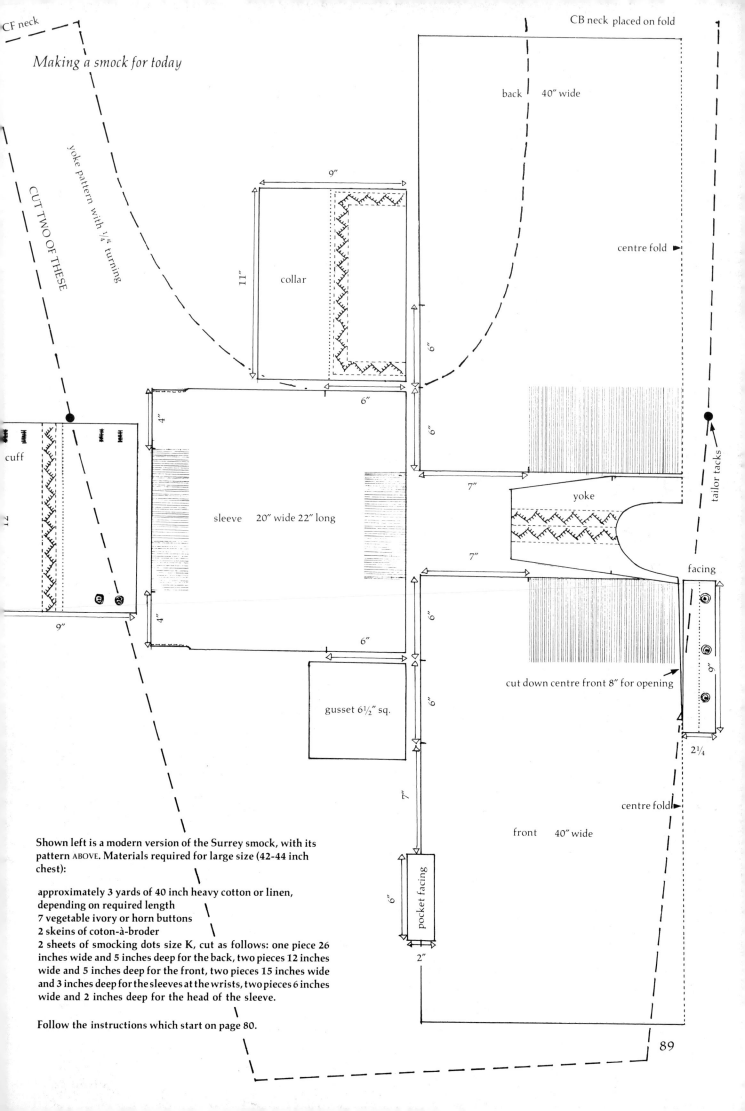

CF neck

Making a smock for today

CB neck placed on fold

back 40" wide

yoke pattern with ¼" turning

CUT TWO OF THESE

centre fold ▸

9"

11"

collar

6"

6"

6"

tailor tacks

4"

cuff

sleeve 20" wide 22" long

7"

yoke

7"

facing

6"

9"

cut down centre front 8" for opening

4"

9"

6"

2¼

6"

gusset 6½" sq.

centre fold ▸

7"

front 40" wide

6"

pocket facing

2"

Shown left is a modern version of the Surrey smock, with its pattern ABOVE. Materials required for large size (42-44 inch chest):

approximately 3 yards of 40 inch heavy cotton or linen, depending on required length
7 vegetable ivory or horn buttons
2 skeins of coton-à-broder
2 sheets of smocking dots size K, cut as follows: one piece 26 inches wide and 5 inches deep for the back, two pieces 12 inches wide and 5 inches deep for the front, two pieces 15 inches wide and 3 inches deep for the sleeves at the wrists, two pieces 6 inches wide and 2 inches deep for the head of the sleeve.

Follow the instructions which start on page 80.

Children's smocks

Paintings including children's clothing from the sixteenth century show garments that were restricting and quite impractical for childlike activities. An unimaginable discomfort was forced upon the sons of nobility. The earlier Saxon and medieval boy of all levels of society was dressed in a comfortable short tunic, which continued to be the uniform of peasant children for many centuries. The paintings that feature fifteenth century children portray them as miniature adults. Girls and boys were dressed in replicas of their mothers' opulent styles; the only recognizable manly feature of the boy's appearance was a sword slung around his waist. Petticoats and skirts were part of his wardrobe until he was six years old, when he would be 'breeched' and removed from his mother's charge. The abrupt change from infancy to manhood was celebrated when the small boy adopted the fashions of his father.

The age for 'breeching' became younger as centuries passed and the transition from childhood to manhood grew less severe. Whilst the boys wore petticoats, the girls wore smocks like their mothers' undergarment, visible and decorated at the neck and cuffs. It was the children of privileged families who were painted and whose images have come down to us, often as manikins in formal dress — but most of the population was rural and they and their children wore the timeless peasant style of tunic or smock. There is some evidence that the garment of the peasant child was occasionally adopted for children of higher ranks for their recreation, thus creating the first step towards a recognized style of clothing for children in the form of a simple smock.

The Victorian period saw little improvement for the health and comfort of the unfortunate child of the middle and upper classes, clad to excess in the

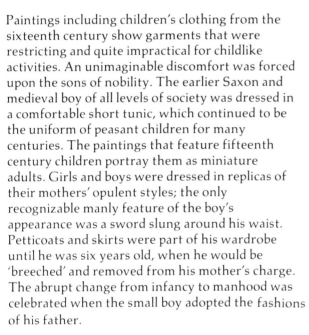

fashion of that period. The unrecorded child of humble origins must surely have had a less restricting and happier childhood and his freedom was reflected in his mode of dress. In his journal *Rural Rides* of 1830 William Cobbett records meeting at Billingshurst in Sussex the son of the landlady of a 'decent public-house' who was 'just such a chap as I was at his age and dressed just in the same sort of way, his main garment being a blue smock-frock, faded from wear and mended with pieces of new stuff, and, of course not faded.' The sight of the smock-clad boy brought back to Cobbett many recollections of his Surrey childhood on his father's farm in the previous century.

Country boys both in southern England and western France wore a blue smock cut in the 'shirt' or 'Surrey' style as worn by the child William Cobbett in the late 1760s. Boys played an active part in the running of the farms and it was

A child's smock of white linen dated 1870.

A round smock of heavy cotton drill for a child, purchased at Williton in Somerset at the beginning of the century. The sale label has '3/4 boys — 15 nls' printed and '13/-' (55p) written in ink.

natural for them to be clad in a smaller edition of the smock-frock of their adulthood. All the features and characteristics of their fathers' protective smock that made it so practical and popular also appeared on the boys' garments. An added feature was the deep tucks in the skirt, enabling the smock to be lengthened.

There must have been many smocks made for boys but few have remained intact. In 1824 Mary Russell Mitford, describing the attire of a humble youth of a village near Reading, wrote with feeling of 'the lamentable state of that patched round frock' in her work *Our Village*. Smocks endured the wear and tear of a farmer's many children, for they were alternately worn and repaired and eventually finished up perhaps as useful linen rags in the farm kitchen or dairy.

Like the adult agricultural smock-frock the boy's garment also became manufactured on a commercial basis for a short period. The smocking was sparse and the surface embroidery was reduced to its most basic on these inferior yet interesting garments. They too were sold at fairs and in local drapers' or general stores and many unworn garments emerged from the latter in the beginning of this century. The sale label tacked at the hem is still legible on some of these examples and a sizing code in 'nls' appears frequently (nls = nails, i.e. one sixteenth of a yard or 2¼ inches), this size often being qualified with the

approximate age of the intended wearer. The cost of such a smock at the turn of the century was 2/6d (12½ pence or about 25 cents), but this was when the garment was no longer worn as a practical overall by farm labouring boys. In the second half of the nineteenth century 'Country' smocks were the uniform for boys in the numerous village schools and were similarly worn in the charitable institutions for the poor. At the turn of the century, when the smock had become respectable and fashionable, a feminine version was adopted by girls of all ages as protection for their everyday clothes in and out of school.

Fashion decreed such cumbersome styles during the late nineteenth century that the reformers of the Aesthetic Movement and many of their contemporaries strongly opposed the enforcing of these clothes on children. Their own children were dressed in practical smocks and smock-like garments. These styles were not favoured by the more conventional fashion magazines such as *The Ladies Treasury*, which claimed of the smock, 'they are decidedly not becoming to little folks.' However, the publicized theories of the Aesthetics had a permanent influence on children's wear and by the turn of the century children's clothes were being designed and manufactured as a separate industry.

The totally impractical clothes of middle-class children during the late nineteenth century.

Children's smocks

The introduction of the informal smock for adults had only attracted a minority following, but by 1890 smocks were made as fashion garments for girls of all ages. The style continued through many decades with only slight variations; some were smocked at the neck or yoke, others repeated the embroidery at the waist or were worn with a sash. Kate Greenaway, the popular Victorian illustrator of children's books, drew garments reminiscent of the 'shift' or 'chemise dress' of the French Empire period at the end of the eighteenth century. These timeless garments have been worn since by generations of bridesmaids, imitating Greenaway figures in high-waisted dresses of fine Liberty fabrics, with softly gathered skirts and sleeves. Narrow frills around the hem and yokes were also characteristic of her designs. The sun-bonnet of the Victorian field worker with its flapping neck protection became stylized by her as fashionable headgear for children. Kate Greenaway's portrayal of small boys show them either clad in traditional round-smocks, or wearing the masculine equivalent of the chemise dress, the so-called skeleton suit. Liberty's 'Kate' and 'Mab' smocks, which were more authentic revivals of the traditional garment, had all the practical advantages of simplicity and comfort. A large soft-brimmed hat, smocked and decked with bows was incongruously worn with these smocks.

ABOVE and BELOW **Kate Greenaway's romantic portrayal of late Victorian school children.**

Children's smocks

**The Mab smock from
Liberty's catalogue of 1886**

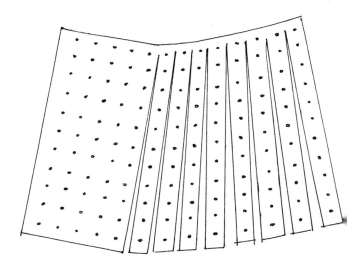

To smock the round yoke popular on baby clothes during the
1930s the dot transfer is cut between each row of dots to
within 1/8 inch of the edge. Fan out these strips with an equal
space between each. Only a shallow depth of smocking can be
worked in this way and a maximum stretch stitch should be
worked on the outer edge. Diagram after Mrs Sandeman-
Allen.

Whilst exclusive markets were served by
Liberty's, mass market magazines gave
instructions for the making of children's smocks.
Weldon's *Practical Smocking* detailed such items as a
'Plough Boy's Blouse' decorated in a similar
manner to the boy's agricultural smock of the
past. The Weldon's garment was described as
being 'exceptionally pretty for boys in petticoats'.
These garments were more fashionably cut with
curved armholes and voluminous puffed sleeves;
there was ample fullness in the body and tucks at
the hem. They sometimes buttoned down the
back and were decorated with 'white work'. This
fine white linen garment, while imitating its
agrarian predecessor, was a fashion smock and has
since become a collector's item.

The publications that followed Weldon's lead
regularly published designs and instructions for
the making of babies' and toddlers' smocks. The
designs of 1920 were typically straight and less
full with small areas of smocking at the shoulders
and hips. Since the thirties the style has changed
very little and has featured the familiar narrow
band of smocking set into a high yoke, puffed
sleeves and a Peter-Pan collar. The yokes and
smocking were occasionally shaped and a similar
version for boys buttoned on to matching knickers
to form a 'romper suit'. In the twenties and

A late nineteenth century fine white linen smock for a child,
heavily starched. This typical reproduction garment is now
highly prized by collectors.

thirties silk crepe-de-chine and shantung were suggested as suitable fabric choices. The identical dresses of the Princesses Elizabeth and Margaret were frequently smocked, and set the vogue for many children of the pre-war years.

Two world wars considerably changed the style of leisure activities, when skilled women turned to knitting 'comforts' (mittens and mufflers for the serving troops). This helped to place hand-knitting well ahead of hand-sewing as a popular creative pastime for housewives. The clothes for children that resulted from the universal zest for knitting gave maximum freedom of movement and were the forerunners of the mass-produced synthetic stretch garments of today. Now there is

A modern smock of heavy white linen; a small version of the smock on page 34.

no longer the need to incorporate into the design of children's wear facilities for growth; modern fabrics have made redundant many past features such as tucks and smocking, for in theory they are outmoded. But in practice, with present-day interest in rural crafts and life styles, smocks and smocking are valued both for their past and present qualities. It is for their decorative charm that the smocked frocks for the children of today are once more sought after for the special party dress as well as for practical wear.

Making children's smocks

The selection of smocks illustrated in this chapter are, like the adult versions, simple to cut and construct. Each design is equally suitable for the small, medium or large size and most medium or light-weight fabrics which launder easily will make attractive smocks for children. As in the nineteenth century, when the smock spanned many years of a child's growth, so these smocks will fit a child for two or three years, with only minor adjustments to the length.

The cutting diagrams are for each size in the appropriate design; they illustrate not only the measurements of each piece, but also the matching-up points for the making processes. The

Baby clothes of 1930

Children's smocks

step-by-step instructions and the hints on sewing methods in the previous chapter apply to these garments and there is ⅜ inch (1 cm) seam allowance unless stated otherwise. Alterations to the sequence of construction for the small calico pinafore are clearly defined on page 102, making this an ideal opportunity for an inexperienced needlewoman to gain confidence and skill.

The small needlecord dress (page 51) for a one or two year old could be equally successful in Viyella, calico or a tiny floral print. These fabrics would also suit the long 'Kate Greenaway' dress, which is medium size to fit a three to five year old. This garment, illustrated on pages 5 and 98, is made in a polyester and rayon blend fabric which has the characteristics of Viyella, being easy to launder and warm to wear. The Laura Ashley cotton prints would also be suitable for this design.

The large smock for a six to eight year old on page 51 is a copy of a shepherd boy's garment and is made from cotton drill. Linen would equally suit this adaptable style if cut to the small or medium size. Open down the front and without the epaulettes it makes an attractive overgarment for a younger child, as shown here and page 70.

The shepherd boy's smock is shown with epaulettes on page 51, and ABOVE without them. Instructions for making are on page 98.

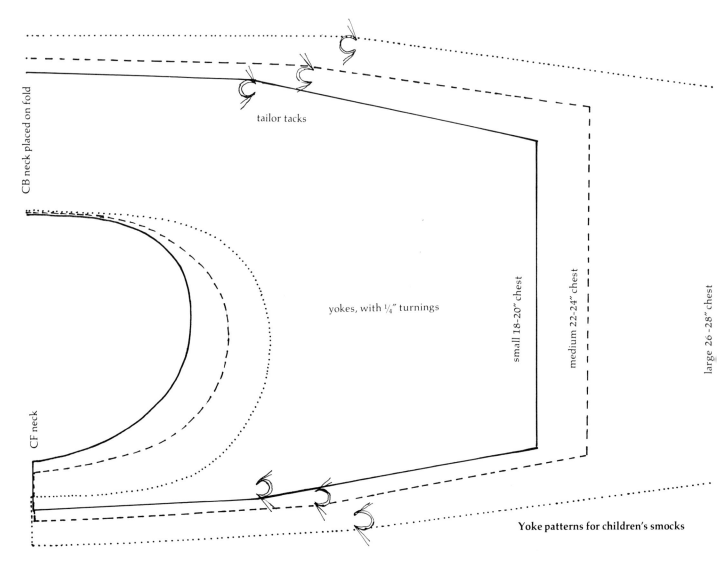

CB neck placed on fold

tailor tacks

CF neck

yokes, with ¼" turnings

small 18-20" chest

medium 22-24" chest

large 26-28" chest

Yoke patterns for children's smocks

Children's smocks

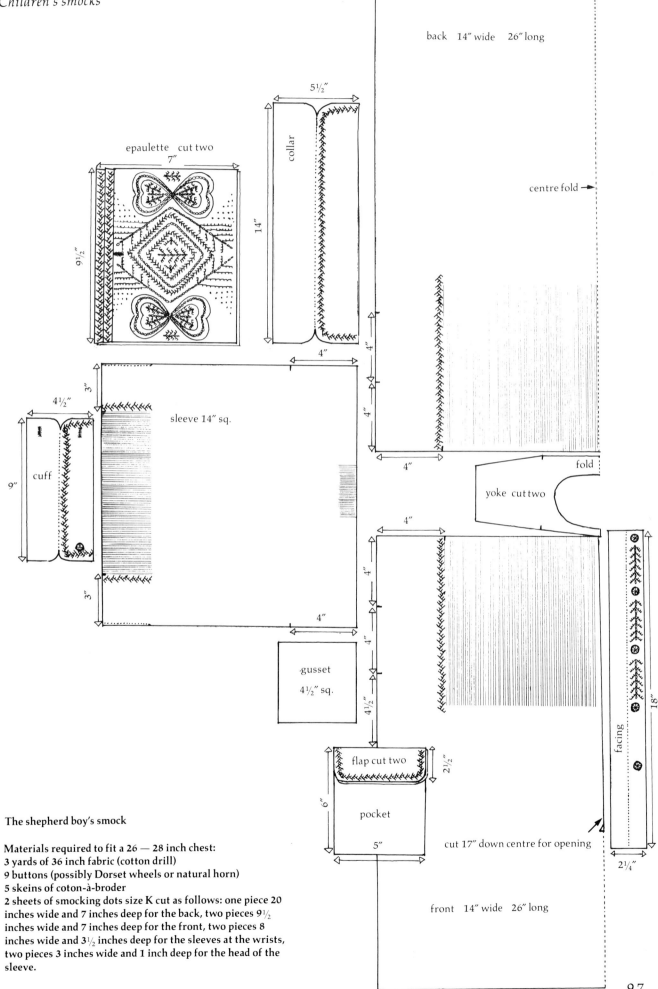

back   14" wide   26" long

centre fold →

epaulette   cut two

7"

9½"

collar

5½"

14"

4"

4"

4"

4"

4"

fold

yoke   cut two

4½"

3"

cuff

9"

sleeve 14" sq.

3"

4"

4"

4"

4½"

gusset
4½" sq.

flap cut two

2½"

6"

pocket

5"

cut 17" down centre for opening

facing

18"

2¼"

front   14" wide   26" long

The shepherd boy's smock

Materials required to fit a 26 — 28 inch chest:
3 yards of 36 inch fabric (cotton drill)
9 buttons (possibly Dorset wheels or natural horn)
5 skeins of coton-à-broder
2 sheets of smocking dots size K cut as follows: one piece 20 inches wide and 7 inches deep for the back, two pieces 9½ inches wide and 7 inches deep for the front, two pieces 8 inches wide and 3½ inches deep for the sleeves at the wrists, two pieces 3 inches wide and 1 inch deep for the head of the sleeve.

5

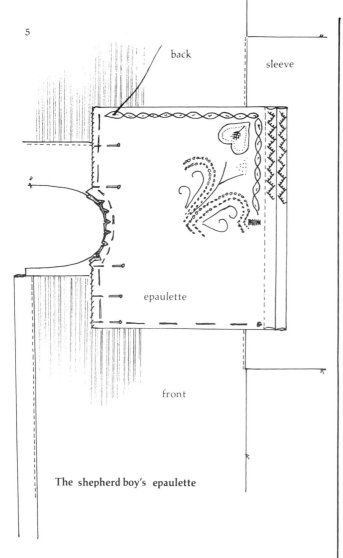

The shepherd boy's epaulette

3(a)

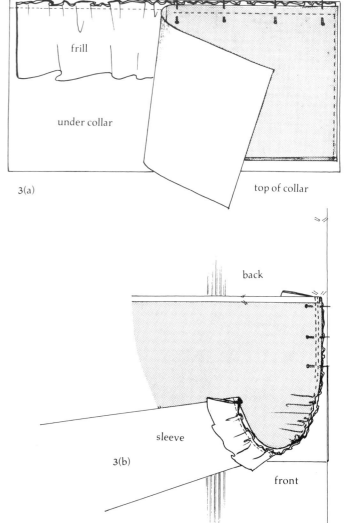

3(b)

To make the large size shepherd boy's smock
(page 51, pattern page 97)

Cut out the material, mark the matching up points and smock the pieces.

1 Embroider the collar and cuffs on the top layer only.

2 Choose and transfer and embroider a suitable design for the epaulettes.

3 Face out the embroidery of the epaulette. Machine ¼ inch (6 mm) from the edge all round leaving a space of approximately 4 inches (10 cm) at the neck edge. Trim the corners and turnings, then turn it through to the right side.

4 Make four good corners and at the neck edge fold out the unstitched turnings. Press it from the wrong side.

5 Follow the step-by-step instructions in Chapter 6 and tack the epaulette to the smock before the side seams are sewn (between steps 6 and 7). Nick the projecting turnings generously so they curve with the shape of the neck, ready to be attached with the collar.

6 The epaulette is neatly oversewn to the yoke and buttoned to the head of the sleeve when the garment is complete.

Children's smocks

To make the medium size party smock (left)

Cut out the material and mark the matching-up points and smock the pieces. Make a tiny hem at the base of the sleeve before pulling it up for smocking.

1   Fold the narrow strips for the frills lengthwise with the right side of the fabric inside and machine the ends ¼ inch (6 mm) in, turn through and press.

2   Work two rows of gathers on the unfinished edge and pull them up, distributing the gathers evenly, until the frills are the correct size.

3   Follow the step-by-step instructions, adding the frills (a) to the outer edge of the collar at step 4 and (b) to the head of the sleeve before step 6 (omit step 9).

4   The frill at the hem is 5 inches (12.5 cm) deep and approximately twice the measurement of the lower edge of the smock. Turn a small hem

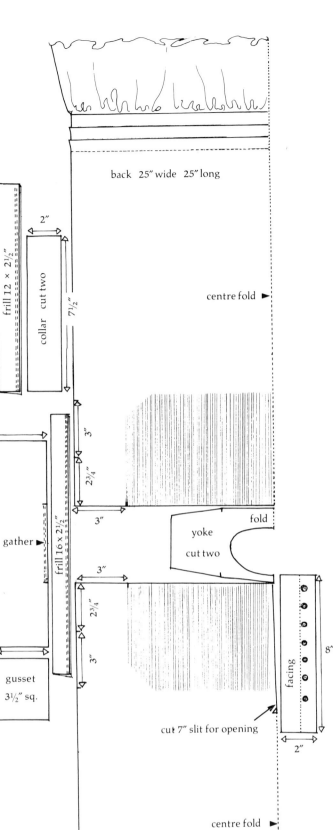

along one long edge and work two rows of gathers (in two sections) along the other. Machine the ends of the frill together before pulling up the gathers.

5   Pin to the finished garment, distributing the fullness evenly, machine and finish off the raw edges.

6   Two ½ inch (1.3 cm) tucks above the frill make the smock 30 inches (76 cm) long and are machined with a large stitch to allow subsequent lengthening.

Materials required to fit 24 inch chest:

2½ yards of 45 inch fabric (Viyella)
6/8 small pearl buttons
2 skeins of coton-à-broder in complementary colours
1 sheet of smocking dots size O cut as follows: one piece 18 inches wide and 6 inches deep for the back, two pieces 8½ inches wide and 6 inches deep for the front, two strips 8 inches wide and 1 inch deep for the sleeves.

The needlecord dress

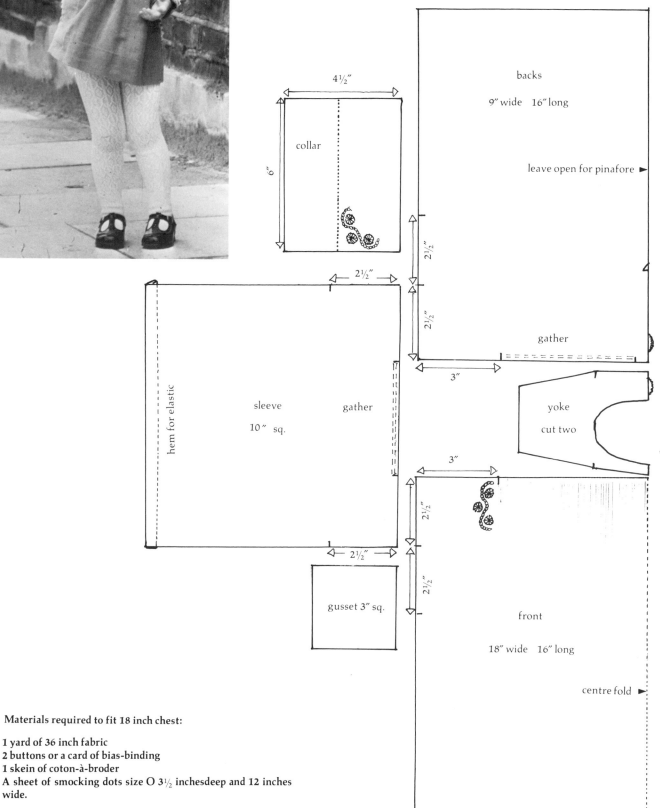

collar

4½″

6″

backs

9″ wide   16″ long

leave open for pinafore ▶

2½″

2½″

gather

3″

sleeve

10″ sq.

gather

hem for elastic

2½″

yoke

cut two

3″

2½″

2½″

gusset 3″ sq.

2½″

front

18″ wide   16″ long

centre fold ▶

Materials required to fit 18 inch chest:

1 yard of 36 inch fabric
2 buttons or a card of bias-binding
1 skein of coton-à-broder
A sheet of smocking dots size O 3½ inchesdeep and 12 inches
wide.

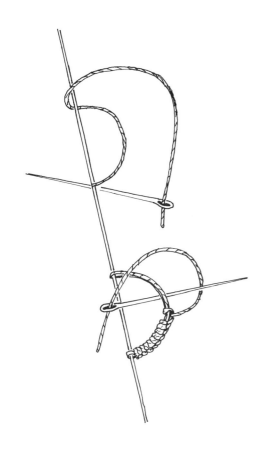

5

To cut this baby's calico pinafore, use the pattern OPPOSITE for the needlecord dress, omitting the collar, and make up following the instructions overleaf.

To make the small needlecord dress (this page and page 51)

Cut out the material and mark the matching up points. Smock the front section and gather the backs and sleeve-head to fit the yoke.

1   Join the smocked front to the yoke as in step 3. Omit step 2.
2   Join the gathered backs to the yoke as in step 3 and use the facing to neaten the back opening. Follow the step-by-step instructions, omitting step 9.
3   Finish off the ends of the sleeves with a small hem and thread through soft elastic, or make frilled cuffs as instructed for the medium size party smock.
4   Join the back seam to within 4 inches (10 cm) of the yoke.
5   Sew two buttons on the right side of the opening and work buttonhole loops to correspond on the left.

To make the baby's calico pinafore

Cut out the material as for the needlecord dress, omitting the collar, and mark the matching up points. Smock the front section and gather the backs and sleeve-heads to fit the yokes (if you want to smock the sleeve-heads and wrists, do it at this stage).

1   Join the smocked front to the yoke as in step 1. Omit step 2.
2   Join the gathered backs to the yoke as in step 3 and use the facing to neaten the back opening. Omit step 4.
3   Neatly bind the neck edge with bias binding, leaving 10 inches (25.5 cm) both sides of the centre back for ties. Omit step 5. Follow the step-by-step instructions.
4   Finish off the ends of the sleeves with a small hem and, if they are not smocked, thread through soft elastic. Omit step 9.
5   Turn a small hem down both sides of the centre back opening.
6   Attach two more ties at the base of the back yoke.
7   Turn up a hem for the required length.

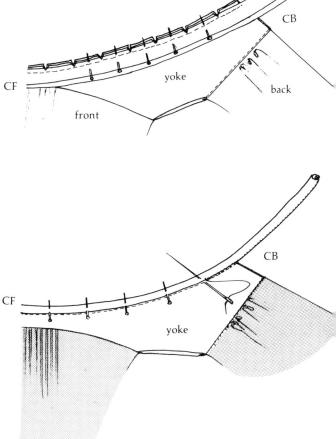

Suppliers of smocking materials and patterns

Britain

Fabric

Linen
Arthur Cordery, Linen Draper, 51 High Street, Shaftesbury, Dorset SP7 J8E
Liberty & Co. Ltd, Regent Street, London W1R 6AH (Liberty's also stock a wide range of silk fabrics, Tana lawn, Viyella)

Cotton Prints
Laura Ashley, Carno, Powys, Wales

Cotton-Drill
Livingstone Textiles, P.O. Box 5, St Michael's Lane, Bridport, Dorset DT6 3RS

Silk
Butterfly Silks (mail order), Acorn Fabrics Ltd., Union Mills, Lower Union Street, Skipton, Yorkshire

Embroidery Threads

Anchor and DMC Coton-à-broder
Mace and Nairn, 89 Crane Street, Salisbury, Wiltshire SP1 2PY (who also supply 'Henry Campbell's Linen Smocking thread (Lintrad) 16/3)

Ruth John Embroidery Materials, 39 The Square, Titchfield, Hampshire

Gutermann silk, Buttonhold twist and Sewing thread
John Lewis Partnership, Oxford Street, London W1 and many other large department stores

Bibliography

Books Featuring Smocks

Armes, Alice *English Smocks*, Dryad Press, Leicester 1972
Ashdown, Mrs Charles *British Costume during Nineteen Centuries*, Thomas Nelson and Sons, Sunbury-on-Thames 1929
Cunnington, P. and Buck, A. *Children's Costume in England*, A. and C. Black, London 1965
Cunnington, P. and Lucas, C. *Costume for Births, Marriages & Deaths*, A. and C. Black, London 1972
Cunnington, P. and Lucas, C. *Occupational Costume in England: from eleventh century to 1914*, A. and C. Black, London 1967
Ewing, Elizabeth, *Fashions in Underwear*, Batsford, London 1971
Ewing, Elizabeth, *History of Children's Costume*, Batsford, London 1977
Lansdell, Avril *Occupational Costume*, Shire Publications, Aylesbury 1977
Oakes, A. and Hamilton Hill, M. *Rural Costume, its origin and development in Western Europe and the British Isles*, Batsford, London 1970
The Workwoman's Guide 'By a Lady', Simpkin Marshall, London 1840; reprint: Bloomfield 1975

Embroidery

Caulfield and Saward *The Dictionary of Needlework, 1882*; facsimile: Hamlyn, Feltham, Middlesex 1974
Cave, Oenone *English Folk Embroidery*, Mills & Boon, London 1965
De Dillmont, Thérèse *Encyclopedia of Needlework*, D.M.C. Library, Paris 1916
Hughes, Therle *English Domestic Needlework*, Lutterworth, London 1961
Knott, Grace *English Smocking*, Muller, London 1962
Levy, Santina *Discovering Embroidery*, Shire Publications, Aylesbury 1971
Morris, Barbara *Victorian Embroidery*, Herbert Jenkins, London 1962
Pass, Olivia *Dorset Feather Stitchery*, Mills & Boon, London 1957
Thomas, Mary *Dictionary of Embroidery Stitches*, Hodder & Stoughton, London 1934
Thomas, Mary *Embroidery Book*, Hodder & Stoughton, London 1936

Smock Gathering Machine

Geoffrey Magnay Ltd, Boulters Barn, Churchill Road, Chipping Norton, Oxon OX7 5UT

Smocking dot and Dorset feather stitch transfers

Deighton Bros. Ltd, Riverside Road, Pottington Industrial Estate, Barnstaple, North Devon
Dorset Federation of Women's Institutes, Princes Street, Dorchester, Dorset (who also supply leaflet on the making of Dorset wheel buttons)

Buttons

Genuine horn buttons
Richard James & Son, 31 Ludgate Hill, Birmingham B3 1EH

Real pearl buttons
George Hook & Co., 154 Villa Street, Lozells, Birmingham

USA & Canada

General Supplies

Little Miss Muffet, PO Box 10912/6709 Glenbrook Drive, Knoxville, Tn. 37919

Ethnic Clothing Patterns and Materials, Ethnic Accessories, P.O. Box 250, Forestville, Ca. 95436

The Smocking Corner, Smock Gathering Machine & Supplies, 2020 Central Avenue, Augusta, Georgia 30904. Manufacturers of The Precision Pleater

Grace L. Knott, 86 Larkfield Drive, Don Mills, Ontario M3B 2H1

General and Social History

Adburgham, A. *A Biography of a Shop*, Liberty, London 1975
Brailsford, Dennis *Sport and Society*, Routledge, Kegan & Paul, London 1969
Cobbett, William *Rural Rides* 1830; Penguin, London 1967
Evans, George Ewart *Ask the Fellows who cut the Hay*, Faber, London 1965
Gaunt, William *A Concise History of English Painting*, Thames & Hudson, London 1969
Hardy, Thomas *Far from the Madding Crowd*, 1874; Macmillan, London 1974
Hardy, Thomas *Tess of the D'Urbervilles*, 1891; Macmillan, London 1974
Hardy, Thomas *Under the Greenwood Tree*, 1872; Macmillan, London 1974
Harvie, C. Martin, and Scharf, A. (Ed.) *Industrialisation and Culture 1830-1914*, Macmillan, London 1970
Howitt, William *Rural Life of England*, London 1838
Howitt, William *The Hall and The Hamlet*, 2 vols, London 1848
Mitford, Mary Russell *Our Village*, 5 vols, London 1824-32; 1946
Peacock, Primrose *Discovering Old Buttons*, Shire Publications, Aylesbury 1978

Magazines and Articles

Embroidery Winter 1961-2 and 1953-4, The Embroiderer's Guild, London
Stitchcraft April 1935, Stitchcraft Ltd, London
Strata of Society, Costume Society publication 1973
The Embroideress 'Quilting and Smocking' Spring 1936, James Pearsall Co., Ltd, London
Weldon's Practical Needlework No. 88, 1932, IPC, London
Bere, Rennie, 'Old English Smocking Patterns' in *Country Life* August 1966
Brown, Martyn, 'Somerset Smocks' in *Somerset Notes and Queries*, Vol 30 March 1977
Buck, Anne, 'The Countryman's Smock' in *Folk Life*, Vol. 1, 1963
Farwell, A., 'A Gathering of Smocks' in *The Countryman*, Spring 1968
Gooding, Kathleen, 'The Smock' in *Country Quest*, October 1967
Jones, Margaret, 'The Vanished Smock-Frock' in *Country Life*, April 1957
Tanner, H. and R., 'Smocks and Smocking' in *The Countryman*, Autumn 1953

Museums to visit

Since the renewed interest in Britain in agricultural artifacts and clothing many Rural Life Museums have appeared, both within the County Museums Services or as small privately owned establishments. These museums are well worth visiting and they usually have a few examples from their smock collection on view. Smocks are generally not well documented and it cannot be assumed that they have remained in the county of their origin.

The following list is by no means a complete account of all recorded smocks, but is intended as a useful guide to those studying the subject. It is possible to examine any garment by writing to the Curator or the Keeper of Costume or Textiles.

Museum and Archives, Abingdon, Oxfordshire Two smocks made for the Great Exhibition of 1851.

Buckinghamshire County Museum, Aylesbury Twenty smocks well documented, and an excellent booklet published in 1976.

Museum of Costume, Assembly Rooms, Bath A large collection of historical costume, which includes twenty smocks.

Cambridge Folk Museum Sixteen smocks.

Welsh Folk Museum, St Fagan's Castle, Cardiff A few examples from mid and south Wales, displaying extravagant and unique decoration. A very informative booklet was published in 1974.

Grosvenor Museum, Chester A coat smock from Shropshire and a round smock from Kent.

Colchester and Essex Museum Eight smocks, including some very unusual examples and many farm-labouring accessories.

Dorchester County Museum Approximately eight smocks, a display of local agricultural trades and some Dorset wheel buttons.

Royal Albert Museum, Exeter Nine smocks, only five from Devon.

Somerset Rural Life Museum, Glastonbury Approximately ten smocks, one very beautiful and unusual garment and some from other counties.

Gloucester Museum, Bishop Hooper's Lodging Eleven smocks, mainly from the Cotswold area, and an informative pamphlet printed in 1977.

Castle Arch Museum, Guildford, Surrey Over twenty smocks, mainly the 'Surrey' type, and some oiled examples. Other fine examples of needlework are displayed and described with the smocks in their booklet *Needlework and Allied Crafts*.

Michelham Priory, Hailsham, Sussex A carter's oiled smock.

Churchill Gardens, Hereford Approximately twenty smocks mainly from the border counties; a varied collection worth viewing. A detailed information sheet was produced a few years ago.

Hartlebury Castle, Kidderminster, Worcestershire Twenty-one smocks mainly of that area; both round smocks and coat smocks made of linen or drabbet.

Victoria and Albert Museum, South Kensington, London A large selection of smocks from many areas, mainly the more elaborate examples, featuring wedding smocks and others of very fine needlework. An information sheet is available.

Wardown Park, Luton, Bedfordshire Twelve smocks, mainly products of the smock-making industries. A detailed information sheet is available.

Newark-on-Trent Museum, Nottinghamshire Several Newark Frocks.

Platt Hall, Manchester Seventeen adult and eight children's smocks.

Stranger's Hall Museum, Norwich, Norfolk Five smocks.

Castle Gate Museum, Nottingham Six smocks, including one very ornate blue example worn by a shepherd.

Harris Museum, Preston A ceremonial smock and one other worn by a brewer.

Museum of English Rural Life, Reading, Berkshire A large selection of smocks from all parts of Britain.

Salisbury and South Wilts Museum Eight smocks, including one particularly unusual shepherd's smock.

Clive House Museum, Shrewsbury Three adults' smocks and three children's smocks, possibly all from that area.

County Museum, Warwick Twelve smocks mainly from the Midlands. An information sheet is available.

Woodspring Museum, Weston-super-Mare, Avon Seven smocks, including a child's revival smock and a fine Newark Frock.

Elmbridge Museum, Weybridge Two 'Surrey' smocks, one child's smock, and an informative booklet called *A Surrey Smock*.

Hampshire Museum Service: Headquarters at Chilcomb House, Winchester. The service has a very large collection of smocks including ten funeral smocks and a child's revival garment. The smocks are distributed amongst the various county museums.

Metric Conversion Chart

imperial	true metric	approximate metric
¼ inch	6.35 mm	6mm
⅜ inch	9.5mm	1cm
1 inch	2.54cm	2.5cm
2 inch	5.08cm	5cm
3 inch	7.62cm	7.5cm
4 inch	10.16cm	10cm
5 inch	12.70cm	12.5cm
6 inch	15.24cm	15.25cm
7 inch	17.78cm	17.75cm
8 inch	20.32cm	20.5cm
9 inch	22.86cm	22.75cm
10 inch	25.4cm	25.5cm
12 inch	30.48cm	30.5cm

Most drapers sell fabric by the metre and the manufacturers are gradually introducing metric widths to their products. The 36 inch and occasionally 45 inch wide fabric is still prevalent for cottons and rayons and 54 inch width for the woollen trade. Synthetic fabrics tend to be wider and come in many confusing measurements:

90cm	35/36 inches
115cm	44/45 inches
150cm	58/60 inches
180cm	72 inches

Approximate metric measurements for the yardages quoted in this book:

2¼ yards	2.05 metres
3	2.75
3½	3.20
4	3.70
5½	5.05